JOHN EXPLAINED

JOHN EXPLAINED

Understanding the Book and Its Message for Today

Samuel Whitaker

Part of the Bible for Modern Life Series

Ascent Press

Published by
Ascent Press

ISBN: 978-1-972885-03-1

Printed in the United States of America

First Edition 2026

For those seeking clarity in the ancient words of Scripture.

CONTENTS

Disclaimer

This book provides an interpretive overview of the biblical text using historical scholarship and modern analysis tools. It is intended to help readers understand the themes, context, and message of the biblical narrative and is not intended to replace personal study of Scripture

Introduction

Why John Still Matters

Of the four Gospels, John is the one that begins before the world did. Where Mark opens mid-action, and Matthew opens with a genealogy, and Luke opens with a carefully composed prologue addressed to a named recipient, John opens in eternity: In the beginning was the Word, and the Word was with God, and the Word was God. No other Gospel stakes its claim this way. No other Evangelist steps back far enough to locate the story of Jesus within the story of creation itself, to insist before a single miracle has been performed or a single conversation recorded that what is about to happen on the shores of Galilee and in the streets of Jerusalem has been true since before there was anything at all.

John's Gospel is the latest of the four and the most deliberately constructed. It shares the basic outline of the others — a ministry in Galilee, a series of encounters and conflicts, a final week in Jerusalem, a death and resurrection — but it inhabits that outline so differently that readers who come to it directly from the Synoptics often feel they have stepped into a different world. The Jesus of John speaks in long, sustained discourses rather than brief pronouncements. He performs seven carefully selected signs rather than the rapid-fire healings and exorcisms of Mark. He makes declarations about his own identity — I am the bread of life, I am the light of the world, I am the resurrection and the life — that the Synoptic Jesus does not make in the same form or with the same frequency. And he moves through a narrative that is organized not around geography or chronology alone but around a series of encounters and responses that accumulate toward a single, explicitly stated purpose: these things are written so that you may believe that Jesus is the Messiah, the Son of God, and that by believing you may have life in his name.

For readers who come to John expecting what they have found in the other Gospels, the experience has a different depth and a different demand. The urgency of Mark is replaced here by something more like gravity — a sustained, unhurried weight that presses from the opening verse to the final chapter. The Jewish argument of Matthew is present but pushed further — John is simultaneously the most Jewish and the most cosmic of the Gospels, rooting Jesus in the traditions of Israel while insisting that what those traditions were always pointing toward has now arrived in a form that exceeds every category available to receive it. The social breadth of Luke is present too, but John's attention is less on the margins of society and more on the depth of individual encounter — Nicodemus at night, the woman at the well, Mary at the empty tomb, Thomas in his doubt, Peter restored on the beach at dawn.

That depth of encounter is the entry point this book attempts to open. Reading John well requires more than familiarity with its most beloved verses. It requires understanding the world that shaped it, the literary architecture that gives it its distinctive rhythm, the theological claims it presses from its opening prologue to its closing commission, and the specific portrait of Jesus that emerges when those claims are followed with the sustained attention they deserve. The chapters that follow provide that orientation — not as a substitute for reading the Gospel itself but as preparation for reading it with the understanding it is designed to produce.

John was not written for the casual inquirer or the comfortable observer. It was written for communities navigating the gap between belief and sight — people who had not walked beside Jesus on the road to Emmaus or touched the wounds of the risen Lord, but who were nonetheless called to the same faith those experiences produced in those who had. The Gospel knows this about its readers. It names it explicitly in the account of Thomas, who demands to see before he will believe and receives what he asks for, and then hears the word that is addressed to every subsequent reader: blessed are those who have not seen and yet have believed. John is the Gospel written for people who were not there — which is every reader who has ever opened it since the first century, and which is the reason its demands have not diminished with the passage of time.

The communities for whom John wrote were navigating questions that cut to the heart of what faith means when its object is not physically present: What does it mean to abide in someone you cannot see? What does it mean to love as Jesus loved when the one whose love is the standard is no longer walking beside you? What does the Spirit do in the community of those who believe, and how does his presence continue the work that the Son began? These are not peripheral questions. They are the questions of every generation of the church since the ascension, and John addresses them with a theological seriousness and a pastoral warmth that no other Gospel quite matches. The Farewell Discourse of chapters thirteen through seventeen is the most sustained piece of pastoral theology in the New Testament, and it is addressed to disciples who are about to be left alone in a world that does not receive what they carry. Those disciples are not confined to the first century. They are every community of faith that has gathered since in the name of the one who promised that he would not leave them as orphans.

Chapter 1

The Human Question

"In the beginning was the Word, and the Word was with God,
and the Word was God."
--- John 1:1 (NIV)

The Universal Search for Meaning That Goes All the Way Down

Every serious human life eventually confronts the question that cannot be answered by accumulating more of what the present world offers. The specific form this confrontation takes changes across centuries and cultures — the ancient world framed it philosophically, the medieval world framed it theologically, the modern world often tries not to frame it at all — but the underlying pressure is consistent: people need to know whether there is something behind the surface of things, some ground beneath the ground on which everything else stands, some reality that does not depend on anything else for its existence and that would therefore be adequate to bear the weight of a human life organized around it. This is not a religious question in the narrow sense. It is the question that every thoughtful person eventually reaches when they have followed the chain of meaning far enough back to ask what it is that gives meaning to everything else.

The Gospel of John begins with exactly this question — and answers it before the narrative has properly begun. The prologue that opens the Gospel is unlike any other beginning in ancient literature. It does not start with a birth or a genealogy or an action or even a historical claim. It starts with a metaphysical declaration:

In the beginning was the Word. The Greek term translated Word is logos — a concept that carried enormous weight in both Jewish and Greek philosophical traditions. For the Greek philosophical tradition, the logos was the rational principle that organized the cosmos, the intelligibility that made the universe comprehensible rather than chaotic. For the Jewish tradition, the Word of God was the creative power by which everything came into being, the same Word that went out from God and accomplished what God sent it to accomplish. John reaches into both traditions simultaneously and announces that the logos — the one through whom all things were made, the light that the darkness has never overcome — has become flesh and made his dwelling among us.

This opening is not merely a theological statement about Jesus. It is John's answer to the deepest human question about meaning and ground. The question of what is behind the surface of things, what gives everything else its coherence and significance, what the universe is made of at the level that precedes matter and energy and time — John answers it with a person. Not a principle, not a system, not a philosophical category, but a person who can be known, who knows those who come to him, who loved the world enough to enter it, and who offers to those who receive him the status of children of God. The prologue is the most concentrated and most daring answer to the human search for ultimate meaning in the entire New Testament, and everything the Gospel narrates in its twenty-one chapters is the unpacking of what that answer means in the specific encounters and conversations and conflicts and finally the death and resurrection of the one whom the prologue has already identified.

The Hunger for Genuine Light

John's prologue introduces a second dimension of the human question that the Gospel will press across its entire narrative: the distinction between genuine light and the many substitutes that present themselves as light without being able to illuminate what matters most. The light shines in the darkness, and the darkness has not overcome it. This is not poetic decoration. It is a precise claim about the human situation: the world into which the Word came was not a world of total darkness, without any illumination at all, but a world of insufficient light — a world in which human wisdom, human tradition, human philosophical and religious achievement had produced real but limited illumination, enough to navigate the surface of things but not enough to reach what the surface rests on.

The people who move through John's Gospel are, in one way or another, people navigating this insufficiency. Nicodemus comes to Jesus at night — a detail that is both literal and symbolic — as a teacher of Israel who has mastered the tradition and found that mastery does not produce what he senses he still lacks. The Samaritan woman at the well has organized her life around a series of relationships that have not provided what she was seeking from them. The man born blind has never seen the physical world, and his healing becomes the occasion for a sustained confrontation about who can see and who cannot among the people who have had their sight all along. The disciples who follow Jesus across the Gospel do so with a progressive and incomplete understanding that is not fully resolved until the resurrection and the gift of the Spirit.

For modern readers living in a world of unprecedented informational abundance — where the supply of content, analysis, and perspective is effectively infinite, but the experience of genuine illumination is rare and difficult to distinguish from its imitations — John's sustained attention to the difference between genuine light and its substitutes speaks with unusual directness. The hunger for something that actually illuminates rather than merely stimulates, for understanding that reaches the level at which questions are genuinely resolved rather than simply displaced by new questions, is everywhere evident in a culture that has more access to more information than any previous generation and has not found that access to be the same thing as wisdom. John's Jesus does not offer more information. He offers himself as the light of the world — a claim whose strangeness is the measure of its seriousness.

The Question of Knowing and Being Known

John's Gospel is more insistently concerned with the question of genuine knowledge — what it means to truly know and to be truly known — than any other account of Jesus in the New Testament. The word know appears more frequently in John than in any of the Synoptics, and its repeated use is not incidental. It is the formal expression of the Gospel's deepest pastoral concern: that the relationship between Jesus and those who follow him is not primarily a relationship of intellectual assent to propositions about him but a relationship of mutual knowledge of the kind that the Hebrew Bible uses to describe the most intimate possible human relationships — the kind of knowing that involves the whole person, that changes what is known by the act of knowing it, that cannot be achieved at a safe distance or from a position of objective detachment.

The encounters that John narrates are consistently encounters in which Jesus demonstrates that he already knows the person before they have introduced themselves. He knows what is in a person — a declaration made early in the Gospel and demonstrated throughout it. He knows Nathanael before Nathanael has said a word. He knows the Samaritan woman's history in a way that produces her immediate recognition: he told me everything I ever did. He knows that Lazarus has died before the messenger arrives to tell him. He knows what Peter will do before Peter has done it, and he knows what Peter will become on the other side of the failure that Peter has not yet imagined himself capable of. This quality of prior and complete knowledge is not presented as surveillance or exposure. It is presented as the ground of a relationship in which the one who is known does not need to manage their presentation or protect their most vulnerable dimensions, because the one who knows them already knows those dimensions and has chosen them anyway.

The question of being known in this way — known completely and chosen anyway — is one of the most persistent and most aching questions of human experience in every era. The longing to be genuinely known rather than known partially, to be received without the management of impression that social life consistently requires, to belong to a relationship in which the gap between one's presented self and one's actual self does not need to be maintained — this longing is the specific form of human need that John's Gospel most directly addresses. The Jesus of John does not wait for the people he encounters to present their acceptable versions of themselves. He meets them where they actually are, names what he already knows, and extends the invitation to a relationship on the basis of the actual person rather than the presented one.

The Longing for Life That Death Cannot End

John's Gospel is the Gospel of life. The word appears more frequently here than anywhere else in the New Testament, and it carries a weight that the ordinary English word does not fully convey. The life John describes is not mere biological existence, not the continuation of the processes that distinguish living organisms from dead matter. It is the quality of existence that belongs to God, the kind of life that cannot be terminated by death because it does not ultimately depend on the biological conditions that death removes. I have come that they may have life, and have it to the full — the Greek word translated full carries the sense of abundance, of excess, of more than the container was designed to hold. John's Jesus does not offer survival. He offers life of a different order than what the present world provides or what death can take.

The raising of Lazarus in chapter eleven is the most concentrated expression of this theme in the Gospel, and John places it deliberately as the climactic sign before the passion narrative begins. Jesus arrives at the tomb of his friend four days after the burial — four days, because any less and the skeptic could claim that Lazarus was not truly dead. He weeps. The weeping is one of the most humanly significant details in the Gospel: the one who is about to demonstrate his authority over death is genuinely moved by the grief of those death has left behind. He does not stand at a clinical distance from suffering and perform the restoration from outside the experience of loss. He enters the grief. And then he calls Lazarus out of the tomb. The sign is not merely a demonstration of power. It is a preview of the resurrection that will follow and a concentrated statement of the Gospel's central claim: in him was life, and that life was the light of all humanity.

The longing for life that cannot be ended, for a relationship with a reality that persists on the other side of death, is not a specifically religious longing. It is the longing of every person who has stood at a graveside and found the standard consolations inadequate to the actual weight of what death takes. John's Gospel does not address this longing with philosophical argument about the immortality of the soul or with eschatological speculation about what comes after. It addresses it with a person who stands at the tomb of his friend and weeps and calls the dead man out by name. The claim is either true, or it is not, and John does not make it easy to hold at the comfortable distance of general spiritual inspiration. He presses it toward the reader with the same directness with which Jesus pressed it toward Martha: I am the resurrection and the life. Whoever believes in me will live, even though they die.

The Shape of What Follows

These dimensions — the search for meaning that goes all the way down, the hunger for genuine light in a world of insufficient illumination, the longing to be known completely and chosen anyway, and the ache for life that death cannot terminate — are not separate topics that John handles in separate sections. They are angles on a single claim that the Gospel develops from its cosmic prologue to its final scene on the beach at dawn, where the risen Jesus makes breakfast for his disciples and restores the one who denied him by asking him three times whether he loves him. The depth of John's narrative is the formal expression of the depth of the claim it carries: the Word that was in the beginning has become flesh, has made his dwelling among us, has been seen and heard and touched, and has offered to those who receive him a life that the world did not give and cannot take away.

The chapters that follow examine the historical world that shaped John's Gospel, the literary architecture that gives it its distinctive structure and rhythm, the major themes that run from the prologue's declaration to the final commission on the shore, the ways the Gospel has been misread, and the specific ways it continues to address the lives of people who encounter it with honest attention. The goal throughout is not to make John easier to receive but to make it possible to receive it more fully — to clear away the obstacles that prevent a modern reader from engaging the Gospel as the sustained, theologically serious, pastorally urgent document it is. John was written for people who were not there — who did not see the signs or hear the discourses or witness the resurrection. It was written, the Gospel says, so that they might believe. That purpose has not expired. The chapters that follow are an attempt to prepare readers for an encounter with a Gospel that does not wait for them to be ready before pressing its claim. It has never waited. It does not wait now.

Chapter 2

Orientation

"These are written that you may believe that Jesus is the Messiah, the Son of God, and that by believing you may have life in his name."
--- John 20:31

A Gospel for a Community of Witnesses

The historical circumstances that produced John's Gospel are not background information to be acknowledged and set aside. They are the conditions that explain why this Gospel sounds the way it does — why its pace is unhurried and its depths are so deliberately sounded, why its Jesus speaks in sustained theological discourse rather than rapid-fire proclamation, why its portrait of belief is so searching and its portrait of unbelief so carefully anatomized. John is a document shaped at every level by a community that had been living with the tradition of the Beloved Disciple for decades, that had watched the eyewitnesses die one by one, and that was now navigating the question of what faith looks like when the generation that had seen is gone and the generation that has not seen must nonetheless believe.

John was almost certainly composed in the final decade of the first century, most likely in the 90s CE, making it the latest of the four Gospels. The community for which it was written was not navigating the acute crisis of Neronian persecution that shaped Mark, nor the extended period of Gentile formation that shaped Luke. It was navigating a different challenge: the consolidation of a community whose founding witnesses were departing, whose relationship with the synagogue had become definitively broken, and whose faith was being pressed by both internal uncertainty and external hostility. The question the Gospel was written to address was not primarily historical — did these things happen? — but existential: can faith survive the departure of those who saw, and what form must it take in those who have not seen and yet are called to believe?

This context illuminates John's distinctive treatment of belief throughout the Gospel. The word believe appears more than ninety times — more than in any other New Testament book — and its repeated use is not rhetorical habit but theological precision. John is tracking what belief is, what produces it, what threatens it, what it requires of the one who holds it, and what it makes possible in the life of the one who does. The seven signs are not primarily demonstrations of power. They are occasions for belief — moments in which the evidence is presented and the question of how the witness responds is the theological center of the account. The extended discourses are not primarily theological lectures. They are invitations to a relationship whose terms are being defined even as the invitation is extended. Every dimension of the Gospel is organized around the question of belief because that is the question the community for which it was written most needed addressed.

Who Wrote John and When

The Gospel does not identify its author within the main narrative. The attribution to John is traditional, drawn from early church testimony that consistently names the apostle John, son of Zebedee, as the source behind the Gospel — a tradition that connects the Gospel to the figure the text itself calls the Beloved Disciple. The Beloved Disciple appears at several of the most significant moments in the narrative: reclining next to Jesus at the Last Supper, standing at the foot of the cross when the other male disciples have fled, arriving first at the empty tomb, and being the first to recognize the risen Jesus on the shore of the Sea of Tiberias. The Gospel ends with a community vouching for this figure's testimony: this is the disciple who testifies to these things and who wrote them down, and we know that his testimony is true.

What internal evidence establishes is that the Gospel is the product of a community rather than a single author working in isolation. The "we" of the closing verses — we know that his testimony is true — signals that the Beloved Disciple's witness has been received, preserved, and transmitted by a community that stands behind it. Most scholars understand the Gospel as the product of a Johannine school or community that developed over several decades, preserving and interpreting the tradition of the Beloved Disciple and producing the Gospel in something close to its final form in the late first century. This does not diminish the Gospel's claim to eyewitness grounding. It locates that grounding within the communal process by which eyewitness testimony is received, interpreted, and transmitted to those who were not present.

Most scholars place the composition between 90 and 100 CE. The primary evidence is the theological development of the Gospel's Christology — more explicitly high than the Synoptics — the apparent awareness of a formal break between the Johannine community and the synagogue, and the level of literary and theological sophistication that suggests a long process of reflection on the tradition rather than immediate composition. The Gospel's relationship to the letters of John, which address similar themes and appear to emerge from the same community, also suggests a period of sustained communal theological work that preceded the Gospel's final form.

The Structure of the Gospel

John is organized around two major sections that scholars have named the Book of Signs and the Book of Glory, joined by a transitional section and preceded by the prologue that establishes the theological framework for everything that follows. The prologue of chapter one is the lens through which the entire Gospel must be read: it announces the identity of the one who is about to appear — the eternal Word, the light of the world, the one through whom all things were made — before the narrative has introduced a single human character. The reader knows from verse one what no character in the Gospel fully understands until after the resurrection, and that sustained ironic gap between the reader's knowledge and the characters' incomprehension is one of the most powerful structural features of the entire narrative.

The Book of Signs spans chapters one through twelve and organizes Jesus' public ministry around seven carefully selected miracles that John calls signs — not primarily because they are supernatural but because they signify something about the identity of the one who performs them. Water turned to wine at Cana. The healing of the royal official's son. The healing of the paralyzed man at Bethesda. The feeding of the five thousand. Jesus walking on water. The healing of the man born blind. The raising of Lazarus. Each sign is followed by or embedded within extended discourse and controversy that presses the theological claim the sign has demonstrated. The structure is deliberate: the signs establish the evidence, the discourses interpret its significance, and the controversies reveal the range of human responses that genuine encounter with Jesus consistently produces.

The Book of Glory spans chapters thirteen through twenty-one and covers the final week — the Last Supper and Farewell Discourse, the passion narrative, the resurrection appearances, and the epilogue on the shore of the Sea of Tiberias. This section is striking in its proportion: the final week receives more than half the Gospel's total length. John lingers here not because he has more events to record but because the theological weight of what happens in these chapters requires more sustained attention. The Farewell Discourse of chapters thirteen through seventeen is the longest sustained piece of teaching in any of the four Gospels and the most explicitly pastoral — addressed to disciples who are about to be left in a world that does not receive what they carry, promising them a Counselor who will remain when the Son returns to the Father.

John's Sources

John's relationship to the Synoptic Gospels is one of the most discussed questions in New Testament scholarship, and it bears directly on how the Gospel is read. The dominant view through most of the twentieth century was that John wrote independently of the Synoptics — that the differences between them were too great and too consistent to be explained by literary dependence, and that John was drawing on independent traditions that ran parallel to but did not derive from the Synoptic sources. More recent scholarship has moved toward the view that John knew at least Mark and possibly Luke, and that the differences between John and the Synoptics reflect theological interpretation and deliberate selection rather than ignorance of the alternative accounts.

What is clear is that John has made deliberate choices about what to include and what to omit that cannot be explained by accident or limited knowledge. He omits the baptism of Jesus, the transfiguration, the exorcisms, and the institution of the Lord's Supper — all of which are prominent in the Synoptic accounts. He includes the raising of Lazarus, the Farewell Discourse, the washing of feet, the encounter with Nicodemus, the Samaritan woman, and the extended healing of the man born blind — none of which appear in the Synoptics. The pattern of inclusion and omission is consistent with a writer who knows the tradition broadly and is making theological choices about what his community most needs to receive in the form he gives it.

The Gospel itself acknowledges that it is selective. Jesus did many other signs in the presence of his disciples, the author writes near the end, which are not recorded in this book. But these are written that you may believe. The explicit statement of purpose is also an implicit statement of editorial principle: John is not attempting comprehensiveness. He is attempting persuasion — the persuasion of a specific kind, addressed to a specific need, organized around the evidence most adequate to produce the response the Gospel is seeking.

John's Portrait of Jesus

The Christological portrait John develops is the most explicitly elevated in the four Gospels, and it is constructed through the dual strategy of the prologue's declaration and the narrative's accumulation. The prologue announces the identity of Jesus before he has appeared: he is the eternal Word, the one through whom all things were made, the one who was with God and was God in the beginning. Everything the Gospel then narrates is the unpacking of what this identity means in specific human encounters. The signs demonstrate the authority of the one the prologue has identified. The discourses articulate the theological content of that identity in the first-person declarations that are unique to John. The passion narrative shows what it cost for the eternal Word to become flesh and dwell among us.

The seven I am declarations are the most distinctive feature of John's portrait of Jesus and the most explicit Christological statements in the Gospels. I am the bread of life. I am the light of the world. I am the gate. I am the good shepherd. I am the resurrection and the life. I am the way and the truth and the life. I am the true vine. Each declaration addresses a different dimension of what Jesus offers and what his identity means for those who receive it. Together they constitute the most concentrated self-revelation in the New Testament, and they are framed in language that deliberately echoes the divine self-identification of the Hebrew Bible — the I am that speaks from the burning bush and throughout the book of Isaiah.

Alongside this elevated portrait, John preserves a Jesus who is strikingly human in ways that the elevation does not erase. He grows tired and sits beside a well in the heat of the day. He weeps at the tomb of his friend. He is troubled in spirit. He thirsts on the cross. These details are not humanizing ornaments softening a distant theological figure. They are the constitutive evidence of the prologue's most daring claim: the Word became flesh. The full humanity of Jesus in John is as much a part of the theological argument as his divinity, because the incarnation is only genuine if both dimensions are real. John's portrait insists on both without collapsing either into the other, and the insistence is itself the argument.

The Role of the Beloved Disciple

No figure in John's Gospel is more theologically significant or more discussed than the one the text calls the Beloved Disciple — the one whom Jesus loved. He appears at the Last Supper, at the cross, at the empty tomb, and on the shore of the Sea of Tiberias, and in each appearance, he functions as a model of the kind of relationship with Jesus that the Gospel is commending. At the Last Supper, he reclines next to Jesus in the position of greatest intimacy. At the cross, he is entrusted with the care of Jesus' mother — a commission that represents the formation of a new family around the crucified Lord. At the empty tomb, he sees and believes before he has received the explanation that will make believing understandable.

The Beloved Disciple is never named in the Gospel, and the deliberate anonymity is almost certainly intentional. He functions not only as a historical figure whose testimony grounds the Gospel's claims but as a representative figure — the embodiment of what it means to be loved by Jesus and to receive that love with the kind of intimate, perceptive, trusting response that the Gospel consistently commends. The reader who engages the Gospel seriously is being invited into the same relationship the Beloved Disciple inhabits, which is why his anonymity serves the Gospel's purpose: he is nameless so that every reader can occupy the position the name would have fixed to a specific historical individual.

Preparing to Read John Well

Understanding the historical context of John's composition, the community of witness that produced it, the two-part structure of signs and glory, the relationship to the Synoptic tradition, the portrait of Jesus as the incarnate Word who speaks in I am declarations, and the role of the Beloved Disciple as the model of genuine relationship — all of these are forms of orientation that prepare the reader to engage the text itself more fully and to receive its argument more completely.

But orientation is preparation, not replacement. The goal of everything this chapter has described is to clear away the obstacles that prevent a modern reader from engaging John directly — the sense that its theology is too abstract, that its discourses are too long, that its portrait of Jesus is too elevated to serve as a genuine encounter with a person. When those obstacles are cleared, what remains is the text itself: a Gospel that begins in eternity and ends on a beach at dawn, that moves from the cosmic declaration of the prologue to the intimate restoration of a specific person who had denied its subject three times, and that was written for people who were not there — which is every reader who has ever opened it — so that they might believe, and that by believing they might have life in his name. The orientation this chapter provides is the beginning of that engagement. The text itself, read with honest attention, is where the life the Gospel promises becomes available to those willing to receive it.

Chapter 3

The World Behind the Book

"God so loved the world that he gave his one and only Son, that whoever believes in him shall not perish but have eternal life."
--- John 3:16

The World That Produced John's Gospel

The world that produced John's Gospel was shaped by a rupture that had been building for decades and had by the time of composition become definitive: the separation of the community of Jesus-followers from the Jewish synagogue. This separation was not a clean break but a protracted and painful estrangement, and its effects are visible on every page of John's Gospel in ways that no other New Testament document quite matches. The repeated references to the Jewish leaders, the sustained controversy over Jesus' identity, the expulsion of the man born blind from the synagogue when he refuses to deny what has happened to him — these are not simply historical reports about events in the 30s CE. They are the literary traces of a community's experience in the 90s, working through the trauma of exclusion by giving it narrative form in the story of the one whose name had caused the exclusion.

The decision to expel those who confessed Jesus as Messiah from the synagogue was not a minor administrative matter. The synagogue in the late first century was the center of Jewish communal life — the place where Torah was read and interpreted, where community was formed and maintained, where identity was secured against the pressures of the surrounding culture. To be excluded from it was to lose not only a religious affiliation but a social world, an economic network, a framework of belonging that had organized every dimension of life. The Johannine community knew this loss personally, and the Gospel's sustained attention to the conflict between Jesus and those who refuse to receive him is shaped at every level by the community's own experience of what that refusal costs those who are on its receiving end.

This context illuminates one of the most theologically significant and most misread features of John's Gospel: its use of the phrase the Jews to refer to Jesus' opponents. In John's narrative, the Jews frequently appears as a designation for those who resist and ultimately condemn Jesus — a usage that has generated centuries of misreading and has been weaponized in the history of Christian anti-Semitism in ways that are both historically inaccurate and morally catastrophic. Understanding the phrase requires understanding that John himself was Jewish, that Jesus in John's Gospel is Jewish, that many of the figures who respond to Jesus with faith in John are Jewish, and that the phrase the Jews in its adversarial usage reflects the specific, painful experience of a Jewish community in conflict with the broader Jewish community from which it has been separated — not a theological verdict on Jewish people as such.

The Greco-Roman Philosophical Landscape

The world John inhabited was also shaped by the Greek philosophical tradition that had spread across the Mediterranean world in the wake of Alexander's conquests and had become the common intellectual currency of educated people throughout the Roman Empire. The concept of the logos — the rational principle that organized the cosmos and made it intelligible — was not a marginal philosophical notion when John wrote his prologue. It was one of the most widely discussed ideas in the intellectual culture of the late first century, drawn from Stoic philosophy and developed in various forms across the philosophical schools of the period.

John's deployment of the logos concept in his prologue is a deliberate act of cultural engagement. By announcing that the logos was in the beginning with God, and that the logos became flesh and dwelt among us, John is both affirming and radically transforming the philosophical tradition he is drawing on. The Stoic logos was impersonal — a rational principle pervading the cosmos, not a personal agent who acts and chooses and loves. The Jewish Word of God was personal and active — the creative power that brought the world into being and the revelatory speech through which God communicated with his people — but had not previously been identified with a specific historical individual. John takes both traditions and presses them beyond what either had anticipated: the logos is personal, is with God and is God, enters history in a specific human life, and can be known in the way that persons are known — not by intellectual apprehension of a principle but by the relational engagement that John calls believing.

This engagement with Greek philosophy was not primarily apologetic — not primarily an attempt to make the gospel respectable to educated Greco-Roman readers by translating it into their categories. It was theological — an insistence that the reality the philosophical tradition had been reaching toward in its concept of the logos had arrived in a form the tradition had not anticipated and could not have generated from its own resources. The prologue is not a translation of the gospel into Greek philosophical terms. It is an announcement that the reality the Greek philosophical tradition was attempting to describe had become flesh and made its dwelling among us, and that the tradition's own categories were now available to be redeemed by the reality they had been groping toward.

The World of Jewish Festivals

One of the most distinctive and most theologically significant features of John's narrative world is its organization around the cycle of Jewish festivals. Where the Synoptics record a single journey to Jerusalem at Passover, John records multiple visits to Jerusalem organized around the major festivals of the Jewish calendar. Passover appears three times in the Gospel and structures its overall chronology. The Feast of Tabernacles provides the setting for the extended discourse of chapters seven and eight. The Feast of Dedication — Hanukkah — provides the setting for Jesus' declaration that he and the Father are one and the controversy that follows. These are not incidental chronological markers. They are the theological scaffolding of the entire narrative.

Each festival carried its own rich tradition of liturgy, symbol, and expectation that John' s narrative consistently engages and transforms. The Feast of Tabernacles involved the daily pouring of water over the altar and the lighting of massive menorahs in the Temple courtyard — rituals that evoked the water from the rock in the wilderness and the pillar of fire that led Israel through the desert. It is precisely at this festival that Jesus stands and cries out that anyone who is thirsty should come to him and drink, and declares himself the light of the world. The imagery is not decorative. It is a deliberate claim that the realities the festival rituals were symbolizing have arrived in a specific person, and that the symbols can now be read as pointing toward the one who has fulfilled what they anticipated.

The Passover setting of the feeding of the five thousand, the last supper, and the crucifixion is equally deliberate. John places the crucifixion on the day of preparation for Passover — the day on which the Passover lambs were slaughtered in the Temple — rather than on Passover itself as in the Synoptics. The adjustment is theological: Jesus dies as the Passover lamb, at the moment when the lambs are being killed, and John underlines the connection by noting that the soldiers did not break his legs — fulfilling the requirement that the Passover lamb remain unbroken. The world behind John is saturated with the symbols and stories of Israel's sacred calendar, and reading the Gospel well requires knowing enough of that calendar to hear what John is doing when he organizes his narrative around it.

Diaspora Judaism and the World of the Synagogue

The community for which John wrote was almost certainly located in the Diaspora — the Jewish communities spread across the Roman Empire outside the land of Israel. Ephesus in Asia Minor has been the traditional location proposed by early church tradition, and the suggestion has much to commend it: it was a major city with a significant Jewish population, it was connected to the Pauline mission that had shaped the broader Gentile church, and it was far enough from Jerusalem that the destruction of the Temple in 70 CE would have been experienced as a theological crisis rather than a military defeat witnessed directly.

The synagogue in the Diaspora was more than a place of worship. It was the primary institution through which Jewish identity was formed and maintained in an environment that pressed continuously against it. The reading of Torah, the interpretation of Scripture, the observance of the Sabbath and the festivals, the maintenance of dietary practices that distinguished Jews from their Gentile neighbors — all of these were organized through and around the synagogue in ways that made it the social center of Jewish communal life. For the Johannine community, expelled from this center, the loss was not merely religious but social and economic, touching every dimension of life that the synagogue had organized.

This experience of expulsion shapes John's sustained theological argument about where true worship belongs and what it looks like. The conversation with the Samaritan woman reaches its theological center when she raises the question of the correct location of worship — Jerusalem or Mount Gerizim — and Jesus responds with a declaration that neither location is now determinative: the hour is coming, and is now here, when the true worshippers will worship the Father in Spirit and truth. For a community that has lost access to the synagogue, this declaration is not an abstract theological proposition. It is a specific and targeted reassurance: the location the community has been expelled from is not the location on which genuine worship depends, because the one who is worshipped has already moved beyond the institutions that organized access to him.

The Roman Imperial Context

The Roman Empire provided the administrative framework within which John's Gospel was composed and the communities it addressed were living. Rome's presence is less visible in John than in the Synoptics — there are no Roman soldiers demanding cloaks, no tax collectors, no detailed engagement with the specific economic structures of Roman-occupied Galilee. But Rome is decisively present at the most critical moment of the narrative: the trial before Pilate, which John narrates at greater length and with more dramatic complexity than any other Gospel.

Pilate's repeated declaration that he finds no basis for a charge against Jesus, his attempts to release him, his final capitulation to the crowd's demand for crucifixion — these are presented in John as a portrait of power exercised in bad faith, of a man who knows the truth and refuses to act on it. When Jesus declares before Pilate that his kingdom is not of this world, he is not making a claim about the irrelevance of the political order. He is making a claim about the source and character of his authority — that it does not derive from the structures that Roman power recognizes and enforces, and that it therefore cannot be evaluated by the criteria those structures apply to competing claims of sovereignty. Pilate's famous question — What is truth? — is the question of a man whose framework for evaluating truth claims is organized entirely around power, encountering the one who declares himself to be the truth and finding that the declaration does not fit any category his framework provides.

A World Defined by the Question of Sight

The world behind John is finally a world in which the most fundamental question is not political or economic or even religious in the narrow sense but epistemological: what can human beings actually see, and what prevents them from seeing it? The sustained attention John pays to the themes of sight and blindness, light and darkness, knowing and not knowing, is not decorative imagery. It is the formal expression of the Gospel's deepest diagnostic claim about the human situation: that the problem is not primarily a lack of information or a failure of moral effort but a condition of the perceiving faculty itself — a blindness that does not know it is blind, a darkness that mistakes itself for light.

The healing of the man born blind in chapter nine is the most extended exploration of this theme in the Gospel, and its structure is deliberately ironic. The man who has never seen gradually comes to see — not only physically but spiritually, progressing from his initial identification of Jesus as the man who healed him, to his declaration that Jesus is a prophet, to his final act of worship before the one who reveals himself as the Son of Man. The Pharisees who have always had their physical sight move in the opposite direction across the same chapter, from confident religious authority to the position Jesus names at the end: if you were blind, you would have no guilt, but now that you say you see, your guilt remains. The world behind John is a world in which the most dangerous form of blindness is the blindness that does not know it needs healing, and the most urgent form of the Gospel's offer is the offer of sight to those who have not yet recognized that they cannot see.

Chapter 4

The Story or Flow of the Book

*"I am the way and the truth and the life. No one comes to the
Father except through me."*
--- John 14:6

The Shape of John's Narrative

John unfolds as a story organized around a single overriding
purpose stated near its end: these things are written so that you
may believe that Jesus is the Messiah, the Son of God, and that by
believing you may have life in his name. Every element of the
Gospel's structure — the cosmic prologue, the seven signs and
their accompanying discourses, the transition at chapter twelve,
the extended Farewell Discourse, the passion narrative, and the
resurrection appearances culminating in the epilogue on the shore
— serves the movement toward that stated purpose. The narrative
does not wander. It builds, with the deliberate purposefulness of a
writer who knows exactly what he is trying to produce in the
reader and has organized twenty-one chapters to produce it.

The theological architecture of this movement is as important
as its narrative momentum. John is not simply recording what
happened in the order it occurred. He is constructing an argument
about who Jesus is and what believing in him makes possible, and
the argument is embedded in the narrative structure itself — in
which signs are chosen and which omitted, in what is placed inside
what, in the sustained ironic gap between what the reader knows
from the prologue and what the characters understand at each
stage of the story, in the way the Book of Signs and the Book of

Glory mirror and interpret each other. Reading John as a sequence of familiar passages misses the argument that only the whole can carry.

The structure falls into two major sections of unequal length joined by a hinge at chapter twelve. The Book of Signs covers the public ministry and is organized around the seven signs that demonstrate who Jesus is. The Book of Glory covers the final week and is organized around the passion and resurrection that reveal what the identity established in the signs ultimately means. Neither half is fully intelligible without the other. The signs establish the identity that the passion will express at its most complete and costly. The passion gives the signs their deepest significance. And the resurrection confirms that the identity the prologue declared and the signs demonstrated has not been defeated by the death that the passion narrative describes.

The Prologue and the Book of Signs

The prologue of chapter one is the theological lens through which everything that follows must be read. Before John the Baptist appears, before the first disciple is called, before the first sign is performed, the reader has been given the identity of the one who is about to appear: the eternal Word, the one through whom all things were made, the true light coming into the world, the one who became flesh and made his dwelling among us. The dramatic irony this creates — the reader knowing what no character in the Gospel fully grasps until after the resurrection — is the primary structural feature of the entire Book of Signs and the engine that drives its theological argument. Every misunderstanding, every failure to receive, every controversy about Jesus' identity takes place against the background of what the reader already knows, and the gap between reader knowledge and character comprehension is not a literary accident. It is John's primary device for pressing the question of belief on the reader throughout the narrative.

The transition from the prologue to the narrative proper is marked by the testimony of John the Baptist, who serves in this Gospel not as a baptizer or preacher of repentance but as a witness — the first in a long series of witnesses whose testimony about Jesus accumulates across the Gospel. The Baptist's function is entirely testimonial: behold the Lamb of God who takes away the sin of the world. He points away from himself toward the one whose sandal he is not worthy to untie, and his pointing is the model for every subsequent witness in the narrative. John's Gospel is constructed as a courtroom in which testimony about Jesus is given and evaluated, and the Baptist opens the proceedings with the most concentrated testimony possible.

The Seven Signs

The Book of Signs organizes the public ministry of Jesus around seven carefully selected miracles, each of which John calls a sign — not because the miraculous element is unimportant but because what matters most is what the miracle signifies about the identity and mission of the one who performs it. The signs are not isolated demonstrations. They are cumulative arguments, each extending and deepening the portrait begun in the prologue, each followed by or embedded within extended discourse and controversy that presses the theological significance the sign has enacted.

The first sign — water turned to wine at the wedding in Cana — establishes the pattern. The jars filled with water for purification rites are filled to the brim and transformed into wine of extraordinary quality. The sign is not primarily about Jesus' power over matter. It is about the replacement of one order with another — the abundance of the new order exceeding anything the old order could provide, offered freely and without condition, at the moment when the supply of the old has run out. This is the argument John will press in different forms across every subsequent sign: what Jesus brings is not an improvement on what already exists but a transformation that fulfills and surpasses it.

The second and third signs — the healing of the royal official's son at a distance and the healing of the paralyzed man at Bethesda — press the claim about Jesus' authority into the domains of distance and time. The official believes the word Jesus speaks before he has seen the result, and the narrative commends this believing before seeing as the model of faith that the Gospel is seeking to produce. The healing at Bethesda takes place on the Sabbath and generates the first sustained controversy of the Gospel — a controversy that Jesus intensifies rather than defuses by declaring that his Father is always at his work and that he too is working, a claim the Jewish leaders rightly understand as placing himself on equal terms with God.

The fourth and fifth signs — the feeding of the five thousand and Jesus walking on the sea — occur together and are placed at the center of the Book of Signs for structural reasons. The feeding generates the Bread of Life discourse of chapter six, the longest and most sustained discourse in the Book of Signs and the one that most explicitly connects a sign to an I am declaration: I am the bread of life, whoever comes to me will never go hungry, whoever believes in me will never be thirsty. The discourse is demanding enough that many disciples turn back after hearing it, and Jesus' response to their departure — will you also go away? — is addressed as directly to the reader as to the twelve who remain.

The sixth sign — the healing of the man born blind in chapter nine — is the most narratively developed of the seven and the one that most fully demonstrates John's technique of using a sign to generate a sustained exploration of the themes the sign has enacted. The man's progressive coming to sight — physical and spiritual simultaneously — is set against the progressive hardening of those who already see, until the chapter ends with the irony fully stated: Jesus has come into the world so that those who do not see may see, and so that those who see may become blind. The sign is not complete until its meaning has been pressed to this point, and its meaning is not grasped until the reader recognizes that the chapter is a mirror in which their own condition is reflected.

The seventh and climactic sign — the raising of Lazarus in chapter eleven — is placed deliberately as the final demonstration before the passion narrative begins. It is the most explicit anticipation of the resurrection, the most searching encounter with grief, and the occasion for the most direct I am declaration in the Gospel: I am the resurrection and the life. Jesus delays his arrival at the tomb, arrives four days after the burial when decomposition has begun, weeps with genuine grief, and then calls the dead man out by name. The sign establishes the claim that the cross and resurrection will enact at the level of Jesus himself: that death does not have the final word, that the one who has life in himself can give that life to others, and that the cost of giving it is something the Gospel has been moving toward from the prologue's first verse.

The Transition and the Book of Glory

Chapter twelve marks the hinge between the two halves of the Gospel. Jesus enters Jerusalem to the crowds' acclaim, Greeks come seeking to see him, and the narrative reaches the moment Jesus describes as the hour for the Son of Man to be glorified. The transition is theologically precise: the hour that has been deferred throughout the Book of Signs — my hour has not yet come — has now arrived, and the arrival changes everything. The public ministry is effectively concluded. Jesus withdraws from the crowds and turns his attention entirely to the small group of disciples who will carry the mission forward.

The Farewell Discourse of chapters thirteen through seventeen is the longest sustained piece of teaching in any of the four Gospels and the most explicitly pastoral in its address. It opens with the washing of feet — a sign that the Book of Glory substitutes for the institution of the Lord's Supper that the Synoptics record, and that carries the same theological weight in different form: the one who is Lord and Teacher becomes the servant of those he loves, and the command he leaves them is organized around the same movement. A new commandment I give you: love one another as I have loved you. The standard is the love the disciples have just witnessed enacted in the basin and the towel, and the love they are commanded to replicate is that specific, costly, self-emptying love and nothing less.

Chapters fourteen through sixteen press the pastoral argument of the Farewell Discourse in three directions. The promise of the Counselor — the Spirit of truth who will come when Jesus returns to the Father — addresses the community's anxiety about the departure of the one who has been their source and center. The image of the vine and the branches in chapter fifteen addresses the question of how the relationship with Jesus is maintained when the physical presence that has sustained it is withdrawn. The teaching on the world's hatred in chapter fifteen and sixteen addresses the community's experience of rejection and hostility, placing it within the framework of the world's prior rejection of Jesus himself. And the High Priestly Prayer of chapter seventeen addresses the Father directly on behalf of the disciples — asking for their protection, their sanctification, and their unity, and extending the prayer explicitly to those who will believe through their testimony: every subsequent generation of the church.

The Passion Narrative and Resurrection

John's passion narrative is the most theologically interpreted of the four Gospels, and its distinctive features are all in the service of the same theological argument. Jesus is in control throughout — he identifies himself to the soldiers in the garden with the divine I am that causes them to draw back and fall to the ground before the arrest proceeds. He carries his own cross without assistance. He speaks from the cross with deliberate intention, entrusting his mother to the Beloved Disciple, declaring his thirst in fulfillment of Scripture, and announcing with a single word — it is finished — that the work he came to accomplish has been completed. The cross in John is not a defeat subsequently reversed by the resurrection. It is the completion of the mission, the glorification of the Son, the moment at which the love that the prologue declared is most fully and most concretely expressed.

The resurrection appearances in chapters twenty and twenty-one are organized around the theme of recognition — seeing and believing in the one who has risen. Mary Magdalene at the tomb mistakes the risen Jesus for the gardener until he speaks her name. The disciples in the locked room receive the wounds and the breath of the Spirit. Thomas, absent at the first appearance, demands to see before he will believe and receives what he asks for, and then hears the word addressed to every subsequent reader: blessed are those who have not seen and yet have believed. The appearances are a sustained meditation on the relationship between sight and faith, moving toward the beatitude that names the condition of every reader of the Gospel who comes to it without having been present.

The Epilogue and the Meaning of the Whole

The epilogue of chapter twenty-one — widely regarded as a later addition to a Gospel that reached its first conclusion at the end of chapter twenty — takes the disciples back to the Sea of Tiberias and organizes itself around two movements: the miraculous catch of fish that recalls the original call of the disciples, and the restoration of Peter through three questions that mirror and reverse his three denials. The restoration is one of the most pastorally significant moments in any of the Gospels: the one whose failure was most public and most complete is not simply forgiven but recommissioned, not simply restored but given a new and specific charge — feed my sheep. The epilogue insists that the resurrection does not simply reverse the passion. It addresses specifically what the passion produced in those who experienced it, restoring not only the relationship but the vocation that the failure had seemed to terminate.

Reading John's narrative from beginning to end — attending to the way the prologue establishes the identity that the signs demonstrate and the passion expresses, the way the Farewell Discourse prepares the disciples for what the passion and resurrection will require of them, the way the resurrection appearances press the question of belief toward readers who were not present and will never be, the way the epilogue addresses failure with specific and named restoration — produces an understanding of the whole that is qualitatively different from anything achieved by engaging individual passages in isolation. John is a carefully constructed argument about who Jesus is and what believing in him makes possible, made through narrative rather than through systematic theology. Its claim is pressed from the first word of the prologue to the last word of the epilogue, and understanding it requires following it all the way through.

Chapter 5

Key Themes

"I have come that they may have life, and have it to the full."
--- John 10:10

The Word and the Incarnation

No theme is more foundational to John's Gospel than the incarnation — the claim stated in the prologue's eighteenth verse that the eternal Word became flesh and made his dwelling among us. This claim is not a theological proposition added to the front of a narrative that could have existed without it. It is the lens through which every episode in the Gospel is meant to be read, the ground on which every other claim in the Gospel rests, and the source of the specific kind of offense the Gospel generates in those who encounter it seriously. The incarnation means that the eternal, uncreated, universe-generating Word of God — the logos who was in the beginning with God and through whom all things were made — entered the human situation in the specific form of a first-century Jewish man from Galilee who grew tired and wept and thirsted and died.

The pastoral and theological implications of the incarnation run through every dimension of the Gospel. The signs Jesus performs are not demonstrations of divine power temporarily housed in human form. They are the actions of the one person who is simultaneously fully divine and fully human, and the two dimensions cannot be separated without distorting both. When Jesus weeps at the tomb of Lazarus, he is not performing grief as a concession to human sentiment before demonstrating power he does not actually share with those who grieve. He is genuinely moved, genuinely present in the grief, and the raising that follows is not the erasure of the grief but its transformation. The God John describes is not a God who observes suffering from a safe distance and occasionally intervenes. He is the God who entered the human situation so completely that he can grieve at a grave and be hungry in a crowd and afraid in a garden.

The incarnation also generates John's sustained attention to the theme of witness and testimony. The Word that became flesh can be seen, heard, and touched — and therefore testified to. The Gospel is saturated with witnesses: the Baptist, the Samaritan woman, the man born blind, the disciples, the Beloved Disciple, the community that stands behind his testimony. Each witness testifies to what they have encountered in the specific, embodied, historically located person of Jesus, and the accumulation of testimony is John's argument for the reality of the incarnation's claim. The truth John is commending is not a timeless philosophical principle. It is an event in history, and events in history are established by testimony.

Belief and Unbelief

The theme of belief and unbelief runs through John's Gospel as its primary organizing concern — more concentrated here than anywhere else in the New Testament. The word believe appears more than ninety times, and its repeated use is not rhetorical habit but theological precision. John is tracking what belief is, what produces it, what threatens it, what it requires of the one who holds it, and what it makes possible in the life of the one who holds it. The Gospel presents belief not as the intellectual assent to a set of propositions about Jesus but as a relational orientation of the whole person toward him — a trusting, committing, ongoing engagement with the one in whom life is found.

The portrait of unbelief in John is equally careful and more unsettling. Unbelief in John is rarely simple ignorance or innocent misunderstanding. It is most often the refusal to receive what the evidence makes available — the decision, taken at some level of the person that is deeper than intellectual argument, to maintain a distance from the one who is being encountered. The Jewish leaders in John see the signs and attribute them to the wrong source or dismiss them as insufficient. The crowds follow Jesus for the bread he provides and turn back when the demand of the discourse moves beyond what they are prepared to accept. Pilate hears the truth and asks what truth is and then goes out to manage the political situation. In each case the unbelief is not the product of insufficient evidence but of an orientation toward the evidence that cannot receive what it is offering.

This distinction matters enormously for how John's Gospel functions as a pastoral document. The community for which John was written was not primarily composed of people who had never heard the evidence. It was composed of people who had heard it, who had committed themselves to it at real personal cost, and who were now navigating the sustained challenge of maintaining that commitment in circumstances that pressed against it. The Gospel's sustained attention to the dynamics of belief — how it is produced, how it is maintained, how it can be deepened through encounter with Jesus across the narrative — is addressed to that community's specific need. Reading John well means allowing its treatment of belief to press on the reader's own relationship to the evidence the Gospel presents, not as a settled matter but as an ongoing engagement.

Light and Darkness

The imagery of light and darkness that the prologue introduces — the light shines in the darkness, and the darkness has not overcome it — runs through the entire Gospel as one of its most consistent and most theologically loaded motifs. Light in John is not primarily a metaphor for general enlightenment or intellectual clarity. It is a designation for the person of Jesus himself — I am the light of the world, whoever follows me will never walk in darkness but will have the light of life — and the contrast between light and darkness is a contrast between two fundamentally different orientations of the human person toward the truth that Jesus embodies.

The judgment passage of chapter three makes the moral dimension of this contrast explicit. The light has come into the world, but people loved darkness instead of light because their deeds were evil. Everyone who does evil hates the light and will not come into the light for fear that their deeds will be exposed. But whoever lives by the truth comes into the light, so that it may be seen plainly that what they have done has been done in the sight of God. The movement toward or away from the light is not primarily an intellectual decision about the credibility of evidence. It is a moral orientation of the whole person, shaped by what one loves and what one fears, by whether one is willing to be seen or whether one prefers the concealment that darkness provides.

This theme reaches its most concentrated expression in the extended night imagery of the Farewell Discourse and the passion narrative. Judas goes out into the night after receiving the bread from Jesus. The arrest takes place in a garden at night with torches and lanterns. Peter warms himself at a charcoal fire in the darkness of the courtyard while Jesus is being tried inside. The darkness is not merely literal. It is the formal expression of the Gospel's deepest diagnostic claim: that the world into which the light came did not receive it, and that the rejection of the light is always simultaneously a choice for darkness — for the concealment, the confusion, and the ultimate inability to see that darkness produces in those who prefer it.

The I Am Declarations

The seven I am declarations are the most distinctive feature of
John's portrait of Jesus and the most theologically concentrated
passages in the Gospel. Each declaration — I am the bread of life,
I am the light of the world, I am the gate, I am the good shepherd,
I am the resurrection and the life, I am the way and the truth and
the life, I am the true vine — identifies Jesus with the source of a
specific human need and announces that the need is met in him
rather than anywhere else. Together they constitute a
comprehensive portrait of what Jesus offers, pressed from seven
different angles against seven different dimensions of human
experience.

The I am declarations also carry a specific resonance that
connects them to the divine self-identification of the Hebrew
Bible. When God speaks from the burning bush and Moses asks
his name, the response is I am who I am — the self-existent one,
the one who is not defined by reference to anything outside
himself. When Jesus uses the I am formulation in John, the echo
is deliberate and unmistakable. The most explicit instance is in
chapter eight, where Jesus declares that before Abraham was born,
I am — a statement that uses the absolute I am without a
predicate and that the Jewish leaders immediately recognize as a
claim to divine identity, responding by picking up stones. The I
am declarations are not merely descriptive claims about what Jesus
provides. They are identity claims about who he is, pressed in
language that locates him within the divine self-identification of
the tradition he is fulfilling and transcending.

The Paraclete and the Ongoing Mission

John's Gospel is the only one that develops the theme of the Holy
Spirit under the specific designation of the Paraclete — a Greek
word that carries the sense of advocate, counselor, comforter, and

helper simultaneously. The Paraclete sayings are concentrated in the Farewell Discourse of chapters fourteen through sixteen, where they constitute Jesus' primary response to the disciples' anxiety about his departure. The promise is specific: I will ask the Father, and he will give you another advocate to help you and be with you forever — the Spirit of truth. Another advocate implies that Jesus himself has been the first — the one who has been present with them, interpreting the truth, defending them before the Father, sustaining them in their mission. The Spirit will continue what Jesus has done, but in a mode appropriate to the post-resurrection community.

The Paraclete's role as described in the Farewell Discourse is threefold. He will teach the disciples all things and remind them of everything Jesus has said — the work of memory and interpretation that grounds the community's ongoing engagement with the tradition. He will testify about Jesus — the work of witness that continues and extends the testimony the Gospel has been accumulating across its twenty chapters. And he will convict the world of sin, righteousness, and judgment — the work of prophetic confrontation that presses the claims of the kingdom on a world that does not receive them. For John's community, navigating the period after the departure of the founding witnesses, the promise of the Paraclete is the promise that the mission does not depend on the physical presence of Jesus or the living memory of those who knew him. It depends on the Spirit who was promised and who comes to those who abide in the relationship the Gospel describes.

Love and the New Commandment

Love in John's Gospel is not a general disposition of warmth toward others or a general orientation of benevolence toward humanity. It is a specific, costly, defined-by-the-cross quality of self-giving that Jesus both enacts and commands, and whose standard is set not by what is culturally considered generous but by what Jesus himself has done. A new commandment I give you: love one another as I have loved you. The as I have loved you is the defining clause, and the Farewell Discourse and passion narrative that follow it are the extended definition of what that love looks like when it is enacted at the level of complete self-giving.

The washing of feet that opens the Farewell Discourse is the enacted definition of the love the commandment is commending. Jesus, knowing that all things have been given into his hands, takes off his outer garment and wraps a towel around himself and washes the feet of those who will betray him, deny him, and abandon him. The love is not conditioned on the recipients' worthiness or on their subsequent faithfulness. It is given in full knowledge of what they will do and in advance of anything they will do to earn it. This is the standard the commandment establishes, and the community that receives the commandment receives with it the responsibility to love in the same mode — not the mode of reciprocal exchange in which love is given because it has been earned or is likely to be returned, but the mode of the cross, which gives without reserve and without condition.

Abiding

The theme of abiding — remaining, dwelling, staying — is one of the most distinctive features of John's Gospel and one of the most directly pastoral in its address to the community for which it was written. The word appears more than forty times in the Gospel, and its concentration in the Farewell Discourse makes its pastoral function clear: the community that is about to lose the physical presence of Jesus around which its common life has been organized needs to understand what the ongoing relationship with him looks like when the form it has taken during his earthly ministry is no longer available.

The image of the vine and the branches in chapter fifteen is the most extended development of the abiding theme. Remain in me, as I also remain in you. No branch can bear fruit by itself; it must remain in the vine. Neither can you bear fruit unless you remain in me. The image is organic rather than mechanical — the life that flows from vine to branch is not a transaction but a continuous relationship of mutual indwelling, and the fruit that results is not produced by the branch's effort but by the life that flows through it from the vine. For a community navigating the absence of Jesus' physical presence, the image of abiding provides the framework for understanding what the ongoing relationship with him requires: not more impressive effort but a more complete remaining in the relationship that is the source of whatever genuine fruitfulness the community produces.

Eternal Life and the Death That Interprets Everything

Eternal life in John is not primarily a future hope for what comes after death. It is a present reality that begins in the believer's relationship with Jesus — this is eternal life: that they know you, the only true God, and Jesus Christ, whom you have sent. The definition is relational rather than chronological. Eternal life is not endless duration. It is the quality of life that belongs to the relationship with God, beginning now and not subject to termination by physical death because it does not ultimately depend on the biological conditions that death removes. Whoever believes in the Son has eternal life — present tense, already in possession, already operative in the life of the one who believes.

The death of Jesus in John is the most theologically interpreted event in any of the four Gospels, and the interpretation is embedded in the structure of the narrative rather than stated as a separate theological explanation. The cross in John is the glorification of the Son — the moment at which the love declared in the prologue and demonstrated in the signs reaches its fullest and most costly expression. It is finished, Jesus declares from the cross, and the declaration is not the cry of defeat but the announcement of completion: the work the Father gave him to do has been accomplished, the hour that has been moving toward its arrival since the wedding at Cana has now fully come, and the grain of wheat that falls into the ground has died so that it can bear much fruit. The death that interprets everything in John is not the dark center around which the rest is arranged. It is the fullest expression of the life that the Gospel has been describing from its first verse — the life that loves to the end and gives itself completely so that those who receive it might have it in abundance.

Chapter 6

Where People Get It Wrong

"The Word became flesh and made his dwelling among us."
--- John 1:14 (NIV)

Treating John as Purely Mystical and Not Historical

The most persistent misreading of John treats it as the spiritual Gospel — the one for those who want depth and mysticism rather than the concrete historical narrative of the Synoptics. On this reading, John's Jesus is primarily a cosmic figure whose earthly existence is almost incidental, a vehicle for theological disclosure rather than a genuinely embodied human life. The signs are read as spiritual illustrations, the discourses as timeless mystical teaching, and the historical particularity of the narrative — the specific festivals, the specific geography, the specific conversations with specific people at specific wells and pools and tombs — as the decorative scaffolding around a message that could have been delivered without it.

This reading misses everything the incarnation is doing in John's theological argument. The Gospel insists on historical particularity with unusual specificity precisely because the theological claim it is making depends on the historical ground being real. The Word became flesh — not the Word became spiritual experience, not the Word became theological principle, but flesh: specific, located, dateable, touchable. John names the jars at the wedding — six of them, each holding twenty to thirty gallons. He notes that it was about the sixth hour when Jesus spoke to the Samaritan woman, that it was cold when Peter warmed himself at the charcoal fire, that Lazarus had been in the tomb four days. These details are not ornamentation. They are the formal expression of the Gospel's central claim: that the eternal Word entered history so specifically that those who were present could testify to what they saw and heard and touched, and that the testimony is grounded in reality rather than in spiritual impression.

Misreading the I Am Declarations as Ego Claims

The I am declarations have sometimes generated a misreading that hears in them a kind of spiritual arrogance — a Jesus who is preoccupied with his own identity and who positions himself at the center of every conversation with declarations about himself. On this reading the declarations are evidence of a narrowly self-referential spirituality, in tension with the humility that washing feet and weeping at graves might suggest. The tension is resolved either by softening the declarations into general spiritual principles or by driving a wedge between the historical Jesus and the theological portrait John is constructing.

This reading fundamentally misunderstands what the I am declarations are doing. Each declaration is not a claim about Jesus' status in isolation. It is a declaration addressed to a specific need, identifying the one who meets it. I am the bread of life is addressed to people who are hungry — not primarily for physical bread but for the sustenance that organizes a life around something adequate to bear its weight. I am the light of the world is addressed to people navigating in darkness. I am the resurrection and the life is addressed to a woman standing at her brother's grave. The declarations are not self-promotion. They are the specific, targeted address of the one who has what the person in front of him most needs, pressing the offer directly toward the need rather than waiting for the need to formulate a sufficient theological question before the offer is extended. The self-reference is inseparable from the pastoral address, and separating them produces a misreading of both.

Collapsing John into Gnosticism

John's Gospel has been claimed by Gnostic interpreters since the second century, and the claim has never entirely disappeared from the history of its reception. The dualism of light and darkness, the emphasis on special knowledge, the elevated Christology, the apparent devaluation of the material world in favor of the spiritual — all of these have been read as evidence that John was already moving in a Gnostic direction, or that Gnostic teachers were right to recognize in John a congenial text for their project.

This reading is historically inaccurate and theologically catastrophic. The Gnostic systems that claimed John consistently did so by allegorizing away precisely what John most insists on: the genuine humanity of Jesus, the real physical resurrection, and the goodness of the material creation through which the Word was made. John's prologue declares that the Word became flesh — not that the Word appeared to take on flesh, not that the Word inhabited a human body as a temporary vehicle, but that the Word genuinely became what human beings are. The risen Jesus in John invites Thomas to touch his wounds — physical wounds on a physical body in a physical resurrection. And the statement that God so loved the world is not the statement of a theology that regards the material world as a prison from which spiritual rescue is needed. It is the statement of a theology in which the material world is the object of divine love significant enough to motivate the incarnation. John is the most anti-Gnostic Gospel in the canon precisely because it insists most emphatically on the genuine embodiment of the one it presents as the eternal Word.

Misreading "The Jews" as a Theological Verdict

As noted in Chapter 3, the phrase the Jews in John's Gospel has been one of the most consequentially misread features of any text in the history of Western literature. When the phrase appears in its adversarial usage — the Jews were seeking to kill him, the Jews did not believe — it has been read across centuries of Christian interpretation as a theological verdict on Jewish people as such: that they are by nature or by divine decree the opponents of Jesus, the ones responsible for his death, the ones excluded from the salvation his death accomplishes.

This reading is not only historically inaccurate but has contributed directly to the most catastrophic forms of Christian anti-Semitism, providing theological cover for persecution, expulsion, and ultimately genocide. Correcting it is not a matter of apologetic sensitivity. It is a matter of reading the text accurately. John himself was Jewish. Jesus in John's Gospel is Jewish. Nicodemus is Jewish. Mary and Martha and Lazarus are Jewish. The Samaritan woman engages Jesus on the question of the correct location of Jewish worship. The Beloved Disciple is Jewish. The disciples are Jewish. The phrase the Jews in its adversarial usage does not designate Jewish people as such. It designates the specific group of religious authorities in Jerusalem whose institutional investment in the existing order produced their resistance to the one whose presence threatened to reorganize it — a group whose dynamics have been replicated in every religious institution in every era, and whose failure is a mirror for institutional religion generally rather than a verdict on any ethnic or religious community specifically.

Treating Eternal Life as Exclusively Future

The most common misreading of John's teaching on eternal life treats it as primarily a promise about what happens after physical death — the guarantee of a blessed afterlife for those who believe. On this reading, eternal life is the destination toward which the believer is headed, the reward that waits at the end of the journey, and its primary relevance to the present life is the motivation it provides for the choices the prospect of reward makes rational. The present life is the place where believing happens. The eternal life is what believing secures for the future.

John's own explicit definition of eternal life dismantles this reading before it can settle into comfort: this is eternal life, that they know you, the only true God, and Jesus Christ, whom you have sent. The definition is relational and present-tense. Eternal life is not a future state entered after death. It is the quality of existence that belongs to knowing God — a knowing that begins now, in the present engagement with the one who is the way and the truth and the life, and that is not subject to termination by physical death because it does not depend on the biological conditions that death removes. Whoever believes in the Son has eternal life — present tense, already in possession. The misreading that defers eternal life entirely to the future loses the most practically significant dimension of John's promise: that the life the Gospel offers is available now, in the specific texture of the present moment, to those who are willing to receive it by entering the relationship the Gospel describes.

Reading the Farewell Discourse as Only for the First Disciples

The Farewell Discourse of chapters thirteen through seventeen has sometimes been read as a historically located address to a specific group of disciples in a specific upper room on a specific night — pastoral in its address to those present but applicable to subsequent readers only by analogy or indirect extension. On this reading, the promises Jesus makes in the discourse — the promise of the Paraclete, the promise of peace, the promise that those who abide in him will bear much fruit — were made to the eleven and are appropriated by later believers in a secondary and derivative sense.

The High Priestly Prayer of chapter seventeen dismantles this reading explicitly. Jesus prays not only for the eleven but for those who will believe in him through their testimony — every subsequent generation of the church, named in the prayer before they have come into existence, included in the request for unity and protection and sanctification that Jesus addresses to the Father. The Farewell Discourse is not a historically bounded address that later readers overhear. It is addressed to the community that John's Gospel was written for and to every community that has read it since. The promises it contains — the Paraclete who will be with the community forever, the peace that the world cannot give, the fruit that abiding in the vine produces — are not promises made to the eleven and extended by gracious analogy to later believers. They are promises made to every disciple in every generation who is willing to receive them in the same posture of honest, abiding, loving engagement that the discourse commends.

Misreading the Cross as Triumphalism

John's distinctive portrayal of the passion — Jesus in control throughout, carrying his own cross, speaking with deliberate intention from it, declaring it is finished with the authority of completion — has sometimes generated a misreading that treats John's cross as triumphalism: a cross from which the suffering has been evacuated, on which the genuine human cost of what is happening has been replaced by a display of divine composure, and which is therefore inadequate to address the experience of those for whom suffering does not feel like glory.

This reading misses what John's portrayal of the cross is doing and why. The control Jesus exercises in the passion narrative is not a denial of the cost. It is the expression of a will that has moved through the cost — that has prayed in the garden, that has been troubled in spirit, that has wept at a grave — and that has arrived at the cross not by having the cost removed but by choosing to pay it in full. The it is finished that concludes the crucifixion is not the declaration of a figure for whom the cross was easy. It is the declaration of a figure for whom the cross was the specific, costly, willed expression of a love that does not stop short of what love requires. John's cross is not triumphalism. It is the completion of a mission whose cost was known from the beginning and accepted in full, and the glory that John finds in it is not the glory of painless victory but the glory of love that gives everything it has and declares at the end that the giving is complete.

Chapter 7

What It Means for Modern Life

"Remain in me, as I also remain in you."
--- John 15:4

Living as Those Who Have Not Seen

The most fundamental practical implication of John for modern readers is the one the Thomas account names most directly: blessed are those who have not seen and yet have believed. Every reader of John's Gospel since the first century is in Thomas's position before the beatitude — in possession of the testimony but not of the sight, called to the same faith that the physical encounter with the risen Jesus produced in those who were present, without the physical encounter that produced it. John was written for exactly this condition, and every pastoral claim the Gospel makes about belief, about abiding, about the Paraclete's ongoing presence, about the peace that Jesus gives and the world cannot — all of it is addressed to people whose faith does not rest on sight and who must therefore understand what it does rest on and what sustains it through the circumstances that press against it.

Living as those who have not seen means, practically, that the relationship with Jesus that John describes is conducted through the means the Gospel identifies rather than through the physical presence that is no longer available. The word of testimony — the Gospel itself and the community's ongoing proclamation of it. The Spirit who attends the engagement with that word and produces in the reader the burning recognition that something more than information is being encountered. The practice of abiding — the sustained, deliberate, returning engagement with the one who is the vine rather than the anxious, self-generated effort to produce fruit that abiding alone makes possible. The love enacted in community that the watching world recognizes as the mark of those who belong to Jesus. None of these are substitutes for a physical encounter that is now unavailable. They are the modes through which the relationship John describes is genuinely available to every generation that has come after the first.

The Practical Implications of Abiding

The image of the vine and the branches is one of the most practically actionable images in the entire Gospel, and its practical implications are more demanding than the general principle of staying connected to Jesus that most summaries of it produce. Abiding in John is not a passive state of general spiritual orientation. It is an active, specific, repeatedly renewed engagement with the one who is the source of whatever genuine fruitfulness the community produces. No branch can bear fruit by itself — it must remain in the vine. The branch does not generate its fruit by effort or technique or spiritual discipline applied with sufficient intensity. It bears fruit by remaining, and the remaining is the condition that makes fruitfulness possible rather than the technique that produces it.

The practical implication of this for modern communities of faith is a specific and counterintuitive challenge to the frameworks that organize most approaches to Christian growth and ministry. The dominant frameworks tend to organize around production — around the programs, activities, initiatives, and measurable outcomes that constitute evidence of a community's health and effectiveness. Abiding presses against this organizational logic not by dismissing the importance of fruit but by relocating its source. The community that is most focused on producing fruit by its own organizational effort is precisely the community most at risk of the disconnection from the vine that makes genuine fruitfulness impossible. The community that most consistently returns to the relationship that is the source — in prayer, in Scripture, in the honest, repeated, unhurried engagement with the one whose word abides in those who abide in him — is the community most likely to produce the fruit that abiding makes possible rather than the activity that organizational effort generates.

Love as the Shape of the Community

The new commandment — love one another as I have loved you — is John's most direct and most demanding practical instruction, and its implications for the internal life of communities of faith are more specific and more searching than most applications of it acknowledge. As I have loved you sets a standard that the Farewell Discourse and passion narrative define in detail: the love of one who washes feet in full knowledge of betrayal, who lays down his life for his friends, who prays in the final hours before his arrest for those who will deny and abandon him. This is the standard the commandment establishes, and communities of faith that take it seriously will find it reorganizing their internal life at precisely the points where the surrounding culture's logic of reciprocal exchange — love given because it has been earned or is likely to be returned — pushes most consistently in the opposite direction.

The watching world will know that disciples belong to Jesus by their love for one another — a declaration that functions simultaneously as a promise and a diagnostic. The promise is that the quality of love the commandment describes, when it is genuinely practiced, is recognizable from the outside as something the surrounding culture does not produce and cannot replicate by its own resources. The diagnostic is that the absence or distortion of this love in a community's internal life is equally visible from the outside, and that the gap between a community's stated commitment to the love commandment and its actual practice is one of the most consistent sources of the credibility deficit that communities of faith in every era have navigated. The love commandment does not produce its intended effect when it is held at the level of stated value. It produces its intended effect when it is enacted in the specific, costly, self-emptying manner that Jesus' own love defines.

Bearing Witness in a Skeptical World

John's Gospel is structured as a courtroom in which testimony about Jesus is offered and evaluated, and the role of witness that runs through the entire narrative carries direct implications for what communities of faith are called to do in the world. The Baptist witnesses. The Samaritan woman witnesses. The man born blind witnesses. The Beloved Disciple witnesses. The community behind the Gospel witnesses. Each act of witness is specific, grounded in encounter, and offered in a context where the testimony is contested — where there are other interpretations of the evidence and other ways to account for what has been seen. The witnesses in John do not speak in a context of general receptivity. They speak in a context of active contestation, and their witness is credible precisely because it is grounded in what they have actually encountered rather than in what they have been told to say.

For modern communities of faith bearing witness in an increasingly skeptical cultural environment, John's model of testimony has more practical relevance than many approaches to evangelism acknowledge. The testimony that John commends is not primarily the presentation of arguments for the truth of Christian claims, though arguments have their place. It is the specific, honest, first-person account of what the encounter with

Jesus has produced in the life of the one who bears witness —
what has been seen, what has changed, what is now known that
was not known before. The man born blind does not argue with
the Pharisees about the correct theological interpretation of what
has happened. He says, with a directness that disarms all the
sophistication brought against it: I was blind. Now I see. This is
the testimony that John's Gospel commends, and it is the
testimony that the communities for which it was written were
called to offer in the specific circumstances of their own contested
existence.

The I Am Declarations and Genuine Need

The seven I am declarations carry direct implications for how
communities of faith understand and address the needs that
people bring to their engagement with the gospel. Each
declaration identifies a specific dimension of human need and
announces that the need is met in Jesus rather than anywhere else.
The practical implication is not simply that communities should
tell people that Jesus meets their needs — a formula that has been
so frequently deployed without content that it has lost much of its
communicative power. It is that each declaration presses toward a
specific and honest identification of the need it addresses, and that
genuine engagement with the declaration requires genuine
engagement with the need.

I am the bread of life addresses the hunger that accumulation
cannot satisfy — the search for the sustaining center that
organizes a life around something adequate to bear its weight. For
modern readers living in a culture of material abundance that has
not produced the satisfaction its promises implied, the declaration
speaks to an experience that is both widespread and rarely named
with precision. I am the light of the world addresses the
navigational need — the need for something that actually
illuminates the decisions, relationships, and directions that matter

most, rather than the abundant but insufficient illumination that information and analysis provide. I am the resurrection and the life addresses the most acute human need of all — the need for a relationship with a reality that persists on the other side of death. Each declaration is a specific pastoral address, and receiving it requires the specific honesty about need that the encounter with Jesus in John consistently calls forth.

The Paraclete and Community Life

The promise of the Paraclete — the Spirit of truth who will be with the community forever — has direct and underexplored implications for how communities of faith understand their common life and their ongoing engagement with the tradition. The Paraclete will teach you all things and will remind you of everything I have said to you. This promise is addressed to a community, not only to individuals, and its communal dimension matters for how it is received. The ongoing work of the Spirit in the community is the work of memory and interpretation — holding the tradition in living engagement rather than in fixed preservation, opening the meaning of what Jesus said and did in the specific circumstances of each new generation rather than simply repeating the formulations that previous generations found adequate.

For modern communities of faith navigating the question of how the tradition speaks to circumstances that previous generations did not face, the promise of the Paraclete is both a resource and a responsibility. The resource is the assurance that the Spirit who attends the community's honest engagement with the tradition will continue to illuminate what the tradition means in the new circumstances — that the community is not left with only its own interpretive resources when the tradition's application to new situations is genuinely unclear. The responsibility is the correlate of the resource: the community must actually engage the tradition honestly and openly, in the posture of those who are willing to be taught, rather than using the language of spiritual guidance to authorize conclusions that have already been reached by other means.

Light and Darkness in Daily Life

The imagery of light and darkness that runs through John's Gospel has practical implications for how communities of faith understand the choices and orientations that shape daily life. The judgment passage of chapter three locates the choice between light and darkness not primarily in the domain of belief but in the domain of love — people loved darkness instead of light because their deeds were evil. The movement toward or away from the light is a moral orientation of the whole person, shaped by what one loves and what one fears, by whether one is willing to be seen or whether one prefers the concealment that darkness provides.

The practical implication of this for daily life is a specific and searching question about the relationship between one's engagement with the light and the actual orientation of one's interior life. The person who approaches the gospel with the genuine openness of someone willing to be seen — willing to have the light fall on the actual condition of their life rather than on the version they are prepared to present — is in the position that John consistently commends. The person who maintains a relationship with the gospel from which the most significant dimensions of their actual life are withheld — who engages the tradition selectively, appropriating what confirms what they already believe and managing their distance from what challenges it — is in the position that John consistently diagnoses as the love of darkness rather than light. The diagnosis is not a moral verdict. It is an honest description of a condition that the light the Gospel offers is specifically designed to address.

The Cross as the Shape of Glory

The most profound and most demanding contribution John makes to modern life is the one the passion narrative presses most directly: that glory and cost are not alternatives to be chosen between but dimensions of the same movement, that the cross is not an obstacle on the way to glory but the form in which glory is most fully expressed, and that the community which follows Jesus is called to participate in the same pattern — not by seeking suffering for its own sake but by being willing to pay the cost that love consistently requires when it is practiced in a world organized around different values.

The hour that Jesus has been moving toward throughout the Gospel arrives in chapter twelve with the declaration that the Son of Man is to be glorified. The glorification is the cross. The grain of wheat must fall into the ground and die before it can bear much fruit. The servant is not greater than the master. The community that has received this pattern from Jesus will find it pressing on the specific choices of its common life at the points where the cost of genuine love — the love that washes feet in full knowledge of betrayal, that lays down its life for friends, that prays for those who are crucifying it — exceeds what the community's own organizational logic or self-protective instinct is prepared to pay. John does not minimize the cost. He locates it within the pattern of the one who has already paid it in full, and he promises that the fruit the dying grain produces is the only fruit worth bearing.

Chapter 8

Modern Reflection

"My sheep listen to my voice; I know them, and they follow me."
--- John 10:27

Questions for Engagement with John's Gospel

The previous chapter examined what John makes possible for modern readers — how its specific teachings on abiding, love, witness, and the cross as glory can be applied as practical resources for daily life and community. This chapter is concerned with a different question: what John does to the reader over time. Not the immediate application of a text to a specific situation, but the slower, less visible formation that happens when a person engages with the Gospel seriously and repeatedly across different seasons of life, bringing each season's specific experience to the text and allowing the text to press its claims toward that experience with the depth that sustained reading makes possible. John is designed to be revisited rather than completed. Its twenty-one chapters contain more than any single reading can draw out, and the formation it produces is not the acquisition of theological content but the gradual reorganization of the reader's interior life by sustained encounter with the one the prologue has identified.

One of the most pressing questions facing modern readers of John is whether the Gospel's depth is accessible to them at all — whether its cosmic prologue and extended discourses and explicit Christological claims require a level of theological formation that most readers do not possess before the Gospel can speak to their actual lives. John's own answer to this question is given in the encounters the Gospel narrates. The Samaritan woman is not a trained theologian. The man born blind is not a student of Scripture. Mary Magdalene at the tomb is not prepared for what she encounters there. Each of them meets Jesus in the middle of their actual situation — at a well, in the aftermath of blindness, in the weight of grief — and the encounter reorganizes them from the inside before they have understood its full theological significance. This is the form that John's formation consistently takes: not the mastery of content followed by application but the encounter that produces understanding from the inside out.

The Distinctive Character of John's Encounter

John's Gospel describes encounter with Jesus with an attentiveness to the interior of the encounter that is distinctive among the Gospels. The conversations are longer, more searching, more likely to press past the surface question to what is actually being asked underneath it. Jesus does not answer Nicodemus's opening compliment. He cuts to what the conversation is actually about: no one can see the kingdom of God unless they are born again. He does not engage the Samaritan woman's theological deflection about the correct location of worship. He names what she is actually carrying and what she has been looking for in the succession of relationships that have not provided it. He does not reassure Thomas after the resurrection by minimizing the demand for evidence. He presents the wounds and invites the touching.

The quality of these encounters — their willingness to go to the level of the actual question beneath the presented one, their resistance to the management of the conversation that the person being encountered is consistently attempting — is itself a formative feature of the Gospel for the reader who engages it honestly. John's Jesus meets people where they actually are rather than where they are presenting themselves as being, and the Gospel consistently invites the reader into the same quality of encounter: to bring the actual question rather than the acceptable one, the actual condition rather than the presented version, the actual doubt rather than the performed certainty. The formation that sustained engagement with John's encounters produces is the gradual willingness to bring more of oneself to the text — to allow the Gospel's attentiveness to the interior of encounter to press on the interior of one's own.

The Signs as Formation

The seven signs in John are not simply demonstrations of power to be acknowledged and moved past. They are formative encounters that yield something different in each return across different seasons of life. The sign at Cana — water turned to wine at the moment when the supply of the old has run out — speaks differently to the reader whose familiar frameworks for meaning have been exhausted than to the reader who has not yet encountered that exhaustion. The healing at Bethesda — a man paralyzed for thirty-eight years, asked whether he wants to get well — speaks differently to the reader who has been carrying a condition so long that it has become part of their identity than to the reader who has not yet faced that question about themselves.

The raising of Lazarus is the sign that accumulates the most meaning across repeated engagement, because it presses the Gospel's central claim at the point where the claim is most personally costly and most personally necessary. I am the resurrection and the life — the declaration is made not in a theological discourse but at a grave, to a grieving woman, in the presence of those who are weeping. The reader who brings their own version of that grave to the text — the loss that has not resolved, the grief that has not found its way to comfort, the death that the standard consolations have not been adequate to address — will find the declaration pressing on them with a specificity that a more distanced reading cannot produce. John's signs are designed to be revisited from inside different seasons of loss and discovery, and they yield more with each revisiting than any single encounter can draw out.

The Farewell Discourse and the Formation of the Reader

The Farewell Discourse of chapters thirteen through seventeen is the most sustained piece of pastoral theology in the New Testament, and its formation of the reader happens at a depth that is proportional to the honesty with which the reader brings their actual situation to it. The discourse is addressed to people who are about to lose the physical presence of the one around whom their common life has been organized, who are anxious about what comes next, who do not fully understand what is happening or what will be required of them in the period that follows. These are not exclusively first-century conditions. They are the conditions of every community of faith that has navigated the departure of a founding figure, the ending of a season that organized its life, the question of how the relationship that has sustained it is maintained when the form it has taken is no longer available.

The reader who brings to the Farewell Discourse a genuine anxiety about the future — about whether the relationship with Jesus can be sustained through the specific circumstances that are pressing against it, about whether the Paraclete's promise of ongoing presence is real enough to organize a life around — will find the discourse addressing that anxiety with a specificity that a more comfortable reading cannot access. Do not let your hearts be troubled. You believe in God; believe also in me. The command is not a rebuke of the anxiety. It is the specific address of the one who knows that the anxiety is real and who has already provided, in the promises that follow it, the ground on which the command can be obeyed. The formation that sustained engagement with the Farewell Discourse produces is the gradual replacement of managed anxiety with the kind of genuine trust that comes from having the promises examined honestly and found to bear the weight placed on them.

The Paraclete and the Formation of the Reader

John's promise of the Paraclete carries a specific formative implication for the reader who engages the Gospel seriously over time: the same Spirit who was promised to the disciples in the upper room is the Spirit who attends the reading of the text in which that promise is recorded. The Paraclete will teach you all things and remind you of everything I have said to you — the promise is addressed to a community whose ongoing engagement with the tradition is the context in which the Spirit works, and the reading of the Gospel is one of the primary forms that engagement takes. This is not a claim about emotional experience. It is a claim about the nature of the encounter the text makes possible: that reading John is not simply the acquisition of information about what Jesus said and did but a Spirit-attended encounter in which the meaning of what Jesus said and did opens to the reader in ways that go beyond what the reader could have reached by unaided intellectual effort.

The formation that this implies is the gradual recognition that the text is not exhausted by any reading of it — that returning to John in a new season of life produces a new opening of meaning that the previous reading could not have anticipated, because the Spirit who attends the engagement is not bound by the limits of the reader's previous understanding. The reader who has engaged John across years will find that the prologue they thought they understood yields something new when read from inside a season of genuine darkness, that the I am declarations press differently against different specific needs, that the Farewell Discourse opens dimensions it withheld in earlier readings because the earlier readings brought less of the reader's actual life to the encounter.

This is the character of Spirit-attended reading as John's Gospel describes it, and it is the character of the formation that sustained engagement with John consistently produces.

The Beloved Disciple as the Shape of Sustained Reading

The Beloved Disciple functions in John's Gospel not only as the historical witness whose testimony grounds the Gospel's claims but as the model of the kind of relationship with Jesus that the Gospel is commending and the kind of reading it is seeking to produce. He reclines next to Jesus at the Last Supper in the position of greatest intimacy. He is entrusted with the care of Jesus' mother at the cross — received into a relationship of belonging at the moment when belonging is most costly to claim. He arrives first at the empty tomb, sees the burial cloths lying there, and believes before he has received the explanation that will make believing understandable. He is the first to recognize the risen Jesus on the shore, before the catch, before the breakfast, before the restoration of Peter.

The Beloved Disciple's pattern of recognition — arriving first, seeing most clearly, understanding before explanation has been given — is the pattern that sustained, honest, intimate engagement with Jesus consistently produces in those who practice it. It is not a pattern of superior intelligence or special spiritual gift. It is the pattern of someone who has remained close enough, long enough, and honestly enough that the recognitions that others reach through extended explanation arrive more quickly because the relationship has been cultivated more deliberately. The reader who returns to John repeatedly across different seasons of life, who brings their actual questions and their actual doubts and their actual grief to the text rather than maintaining the comfortable distance of general appreciation, is practicing the kind of engagement the Beloved Disciple embodies

— and will find, over time, that the recognitions it produces are increasingly like his: arriving before the explanation is complete, grounded in intimacy rather than argument.

Failure, Restoration, and the Formation of the Reader

The epilogue's account of Peter's restoration is the most pastorally significant moment in John's Gospel for communities of faith that know their own patterns of failure, and its formation of the reader happens at a depth proportional to the honesty with which the reader brings their own version of Peter's failure to the encounter. Peter has denied Jesus three times in the courtyard of the high priest — the symmetry between the charcoal fire of the denial and the charcoal fire of the breakfast on the beach is deliberate and unmistakable. The restoration takes the same form as the failure: three questions, three declarations of love, three commissions to feed and tend the sheep. The failure is not erased. It is addressed specifically, in the same number and at the same level of personal cost.

The formation that sustained engagement with the epilogue produces is the gradual recognition that the restoration it describes is not reserved for Peter or for those whose failure has been as public and as complete as his. It is the pattern of how the risen Jesus addresses failure in the community that carries his name — specifically, personally, in the form that mirrors the failure without being limited by it, restoring not only the relationship but the vocation that the failure seemed to have terminated. The reader who has experienced their own version of the charcoal fire — their own denial of what they claimed to hold, their own abandonment of what they professed to value — will find in the epilogue not the comfortable assurance that failure is inconsequential but the specific, costly, named address of the one who meets the failure where it happened and asks, in the same location and with the same specificity, whether love is still there.

The question is not rhetorical. It is the question the reader must answer, and the Gospel holds the space open for the answer rather than providing it.

Chapter 9

Reflection Questions

"Blessed are those who have not seen and yet have believed."
--- John 20:29 (NIV)

Engaging John's Gospel

John's Gospel is designed not to be received at a comfortable distance but engaged at the level at which it presses its claims — the level of genuine belief, genuine need, genuine encounter with the one the prologue has identified. The questions that follow are offered as entry points for that kind of engagement: not questions with definitive answers, but questions that grow more rather than less demanding as the reader grows and as the circumstances of their life change around them. They are designed to be returned to across different seasons of life and different stages of understanding, with the expectation that what they yield will be different at different stages because the life brought to them has deepened and the specific ways John's claims press against that life have become more visible.

These questions are organized around John's most distinctive themes rather than around the Gospel's narrative sequence, because the themes are what John's argument is designed to press and because they are the points at which the Gospel most consistently creates the productive discomfort that genuine engagement requires. They are not questions that can be answered quickly or answered once and set aside. They are questions that the Gospel keeps pressing from different angles across its twenty-one chapters, and that the reader who engages them honestly will find pressing back from different angles across their own life. The goal is not the completion of a set of reflection exercises but the kind of sustained, honest, repeatedly renewed engagement with the text that John was written to produce.

On the Prologue and Belief

John's prologue declares that the eternal Word became flesh and made his dwelling among us before a single sign has been performed or a single conversation recorded. What difference does it make to receive the prologue's claim as genuinely true — that the logos through whom all things were made entered human history in the specific person of Jesus of Nazareth — rather than as an inspiring theological framework that one holds at a certain intellectual distance? Where in your own engagement with the prologue is the gap between acknowledging its content and genuinely believing it most visible and most honest?

The Gospel states its purpose near its end: these things are written so that you may believe that Jesus is the Messiah, the Son of God, and that by believing you may have life in his name. Do you believe this — not as a general religious affiliation or a cultural inheritance, but in the specific, relational, whole-person sense that John means by the word believe? Where is your belief most solid, and where is it most pressed? What are the specific circumstances of your life that most consistently test the belief John is seeking to produce, and what does your response to those circumstances reveal about the actual condition of your belief?

John's Jesus says to Thomas: because you have seen me, you have believed; blessed are those who have not seen and yet have believed. You are in Thomas's position before the beatitude. You have not seen. You have the testimony — the Gospel itself and the community that has transmitted it. What is the relationship between the testimony you have received and the belief the Gospel is calling you to? Where does the testimony feel adequate to the weight you are placing on it, and where does it feel thin? And what would it mean to press on the testimony honestly — to investigate it with the same seriousness that Luke commended in his prologue — rather than either dismissing it or accepting it without examination?

On the Signs and Genuine Need

The seven signs in John are organized around seven dimensions of human need, each addressed by Jesus' specific action and followed by discourse that presses the theological significance of what has happened. Before engaging the specific signs, the foundational question must be asked honestly: which of the seven most closely corresponds to the specific need you are carrying at this stage of your life? Not which you would most like to receive, but which most accurately names the condition you are actually in. The answer to this question shapes everything about how the sign that corresponds to it will speak.

The man at Bethesda has been paralyzed for thirty-eight years. Jesus asks him: do you want to get well? The question is not sarcastic. It is the most serious question that can be asked of someone who has been in a condition long enough that the condition has become part of their identity — who has organized their life, their expectations, their relationships, and their sense of what is possible around the assumption that the condition is permanent. What is the condition you have been carrying long enough that you have stopped asking whether it can change? And what would it mean to receive Jesus' question to the paralyzed man as a question addressed to you specifically, in the specific form your condition takes?

The raising of Lazarus is the climactic sign, placed by John immediately before the passion narrative begins. Jesus declares: I am the resurrection and the life. Whoever believes in me will live, even though they die. Martha receives this declaration at her brother's grave — in the specific, unmanageable weight of actual loss, not in a theological seminar where the proposition can be evaluated at a comfortable distance. Have you received this declaration in the way Martha received it — standing at a grave, carrying a grief that the standard consolations have not been adequate to address? What does the declaration mean to you in that specific location, and how does receiving it there differ from receiving it in a context where the claim is not yet personally costly?

On the I Am Declarations and Self-Examination

The seven I am declarations each address a specific dimension of human need and invite honest self-examination about the actual condition one is bringing to the encounter. I am the bread of life — whoever comes to me will never go hungry. Before engaging this declaration, the honest question must be asked: what is the specific thing you are most hungry for that the accumulation of what the surrounding world provides has not satisfied? Not hunger in general, but the specific, identifiable absence that organizes your sense of what is still missing from a life that has, by most external measures, enough. The declaration is addressed to that specific hunger, and receiving it requires naming the hunger honestly enough to recognize what is being offered.

I am the light of the world — whoever follows me will never walk in darkness. The judgment passage of chapter three locates the choice between light and darkness in the domain of love: people loved darkness instead of light because their deeds were evil. Where in your own life is there a preference for the concealment that darkness provides — a dimension of your actual life that you manage your distance from the light in order to protect? The question is not a moral accusation. It is the diagnostic question that the declaration itself generates: the light is available, the offer is open, and the question is whether you are approaching it with the genuine openness of someone willing to be seen.

I am the resurrection and the life — this declaration addresses the deepest human need of all. Where in your own experience is the need for a reality that persists on the other side of death — not as an abstract consolation for a distant future event but as the present ground of a life that is not organized around the avoidance of what death takes? The declaration is not primarily about what happens after you die. It is about whether the relationship with Jesus that John describes is real enough, and present enough, to organize your current existence around a center that death cannot remove. Is it? And if not, what would need to change in the actual texture of your daily life for it to become so?

On the Farewell Discourse and Abiding

The Farewell Discourse opens with a command: do not let your hearts be troubled. You believe in God; believe also in me. The command is addressed to people whose anxiety is real and whose circumstances warrant it — they are about to lose the physical presence of the one around whom their common life has been organized. Where in your own life is there a genuine anxiety about the future that corresponds to the disciples' situation in the upper room? Not anxiety in general, but the specific form that the uncertainty about what comes next takes in the specific circumstances you are currently navigating. The command is addressed to that specific anxiety, and receiving it requires naming the anxiety honestly enough to recognize what is being promised in response to it.

The image of the vine and the branches is the most concentrated expression of the abiding theme. Remain in me, as I also remain in you. No branch can bear fruit by itself. The image invites honest examination of the actual practice of remaining —

not the intention to remain or the general orientation toward remaining, but the specific, observable practice of the returning, unhurried, non-instrumental engagement with Jesus that abiding requires. Where in your daily life is there evidence of genuine abiding — of the kind of sustained, specific, returning engagement with the one who is the vine that the image is describing? And where is what presents itself as spiritual engagement actually the organizational effort to produce fruit by other means, disconnected from the relationship that is the only source of genuine fruitfulness?

The High Priestly Prayer of chapter seventeen includes you by name — or rather, by description. Jesus prays for those who will believe in him through the disciples' testimony. You are among those for whom he prays: that you may be one, as he and the Father are one; that you may have the full measure of his joy; that you may be sanctified by the truth; that you may be with him where he is. Have you received this prayer as addressed to you specifically? Not as a general theological fact about the scope of the atonement but as the specific intercession of the one who prays for you in full knowledge of what you are and what you will need. What does receiving it specifically change about how you understand your relationship with the one who is praying?

On Love and the Community

The new commandment — love one another as I have loved you — sets a standard defined by the washing of feet and the cross rather than by the general cultural understanding of love as warmth and goodwill. Before engaging the specific ways the commandment presses on community life, the honest question must be asked: do you love the specific people in your specific community in the way Jesus' love of his disciples defines? Not in general — specifically. The disciples Jesus washed feet for included the one who would betray him, the one who would deny him three times, and the ones who would abandon him at the arrest. The love the commandment establishes is given in full knowledge of what the recipients will do and without the condition of their subsequent faithfulness. Is the love you practice in your community of that kind? And where is there the largest gap between the standard the commandment sets and the love your community actually produces?

By this everyone will know that you are my disciples, if you love one another. The declaration functions as both promise and diagnostic. Where in the life of your community is the quality of love between its members recognizable from the outside as something the surrounding culture does not produce and cannot replicate? And where is the gap between the stated commitment to the love commandment and the observable practice of love in the community's actual life most visible and most consequential for its credibility in the world it is embedded in? The question is not a call to self-condemnation. It is the practical pressing of a command whose fulfillment the Gospel identifies as the primary mark of genuine discipleship.

On the Passion and Glory

John presents the cross as the glorification of the Son — the moment at which the love declared in the prologue and demonstrated in the signs reaches its fullest and most costly expression. It is finished is not the cry of defeat but the announcement of completion. Where in your own engagement with the passion narrative is it most difficult to receive the cross as glorification rather than as tragedy interrupted by resurrection? The question is not whether the cross involved genuine suffering — it did — but whether the suffering and the glory are dimensions of the same movement rather than alternatives between which the narrative must choose. What would it mean for your understanding of the cross to receive John's interpretation of it fully rather than softening it into a more comfortable form?

The grain of wheat must fall into the ground and die before it can bear much fruit. This image is not primarily about martyrdom or exceptional sacrifice. It is about the pattern of the life that genuine love produces in those who practice it consistently — the pattern of giving that does not reserve enough for self-protection, of serving that moves toward cost rather than away from it, of the kind of love that lays down its life for its friends. Where in your own discipleship is the grain of wheat most clearly at the surface — where the cost of the love the Gospel commends is most specific and most identifiable? And what does your response to that cost reveal about the actual orientation of your life around the pattern the cross defines?

On Witness and Being Known

The man born blind offers the most direct model of witness in the Gospel: I was blind. Now I see. The testimony is specific, first-person, grounded in encounter, and offered in a context of active contestation without either apology or argument. What is your equivalent of this testimony — the specific, identifiable thing that has changed in your own life through the encounter with Jesus that the Gospel describes? Not what you believe about Jesus in the abstract, but what is different about the specific texture of your daily existence because of the relationship the Gospel commends. The testimony that John models is not primarily an argument for the truth of Christian claims. It is the honest, specific account of what genuine encounter produces in the one who experiences it.

Questions for Continued Engagement

These questions are a beginning rather than an ending. John's Gospel is designed to generate more searching engagement the more honestly it is read — not because it is obscure but because it is deep, and depth yields more to each return than any single engagement can draw out. The reader who returns to John in six months or a year will find that these questions have not been answered and set aside but have deepened and shifted, because the life they are asked about has changed and because different dimensions of the Gospel's argument have become newly pressing in the new circumstances.

The most important thing about these questions is not that they be answered definitively but that they be taken seriously with the quality of engagement that John's own encounters model: the willingness to bring the actual question beneath the presented one, the actual condition rather than the acceptable version, the actual doubt rather than the performed certainty. The person who engages John this way — who does not settle for the comfort of a distanced appreciation when the demanding encounter is what the text actually offers — is practicing the kind of engagement the Gospel was written to produce. Not the engagement of those who hear and admire and maintain their distance, but the engagement of those who hear and are reorganized from the inside, who find over time that the text has done something to them that they did not plan and could not have managed by their own effort. This is what John does to the reader who brings sufficient honesty to the encounter. It is what it has always done. It is what it does now.

Chapter 10

Five Lessons

*"In the beginning was the Word, and the Word was with God,
and the Word was God."*
--- John 1:1

Five Lessons from John's Gospel

The capacity of John's Gospel to shape communities of faith has
not diminished across nearly two thousand years of engagement.
The Gospel that begins before creation and ends on a beach at
dawn has proven capable of addressing communities as different
from one another as the Johannine communities of the late first
century, the Nicene councils that drew on its Christology to
articulate the doctrine of the Trinity, the mystics of the medieval
period who found in its language of abiding and indwelling the
vocabulary for their contemplative experience, and the diverse
communities of faith navigating the contemporary world. The
reason is not that the Gospel is vague enough to mean anything to
anyone. It is that the specific claims it makes — that the eternal
Word became flesh, that believing in him produces life, that love
defined by the cross is the mark of genuine discipleship, that the
Paraclete sustains the mission in every generation — address
dimensions of human experience and community life that do not
change with the century or the culture.

The five lessons that follow are not a summary of John's
content. They are a distillation of the most persistent and most
demanding things the Gospel asks of those who receive it — the
things that remain pressing after all the historical context has been
provided, all the structural features have been explained, all the

theological categories have been identified. They are the lessons that remain when the reader has finished absorbing the information the Gospel provides and is left with the question the information has been building toward from the prologue's first verse: do you believe? Each lesson is an answer to that question from a different angle, and together they constitute the response that John has been pressing its readers toward from the cosmic declaration of the opening to the intimate restoration of the closing.

Lesson One: The Word Became Flesh and Nothing Is the Same

John's most fundamental and most far-reaching lesson is the one stated in the eighteenth verse of the first chapter and unpacked across the twenty-one chapters that follow: the Word became flesh and made his dwelling among us. This is not a theological proposition about the metaphysics of the Trinity, though it has implications for that. It is not a claim about the mechanism by which salvation is accomplished, though it has implications for that as well. It is the most concentrated statement of the most radical claim that can be made about the relationship between God and the material world: that the eternal, uncreated, universe-generating logos entered the human situation so completely that he could grow tired beside a well, weep at a grave, and feel the nails. And that this entry changes everything about what it means to be human, to suffer, to die, and to seek the God who is not now at a safe distance from any of those experiences.

The practical implications of this lesson extend into every domain of life that the incarnation touches — which is every domain, since the Word became not a spiritual experience or a theological category but flesh. The God of John's Gospel is not a God who observes the human situation from outside and occasionally intervenes. He is the God who entered it so specifically that those who were present could touch what they had seen and heard and testify to it. This means that no dimension of human experience is outside the scope of what the incarnation has entered: not the exhaustion, not the grief, not the fear in the garden, not the physical agony of the cross. The formation that sustained engagement with this lesson produces is the gradual replacement of a God who is abstractly present with a God who is concretely near — present to the specific texture of daily experience in the way that the Word's becoming flesh makes possible and that no other theology of divine presence can quite replicate.

The lesson also carries a specific implication for how communities of faith understand their embodied common life. If the Word became flesh, then the physical, material, socially embedded dimensions of the community's life are not obstacles to the spiritual mission but the medium through which it is conducted. The washing of feet is not a spiritual illustration enacted in physical form. It is a physical action with theological meaning inseparable from its physicality — meaning that evaporates if the foot-washing is allegorized into a general principle of humility rather than received as a specific, costly, embodied enactment of what love looks like when it is practiced at the level the incarnation establishes. The community that has received this lesson will find it pressing on the specific, physical, embodied practices of its common life in ways that a community organized primarily around abstract spiritual engagement does not encounter.

Lesson Two: Belief Is the Work

John's second lesson is the one that the Gospel states most explicitly in its account of the crowd's question to Jesus: what must we do to do the works God requires? The answer is the most concentrated and most disorienting answer to that question in the New Testament: the work of God is this — to believe in the one he has sent. Belief is not the precondition for the work. It is the work. The entire restructuring of the community's activity around the production of outcomes that can be measured and evaluated and reported is challenged at its foundation by this declaration: the primary thing the Gospel requires is not activity but orientation — the sustained, whole-person engagement of the self with the one in whom life is found.

This lesson is among John's most counterintuitive and most consistently resisted contributions to the life of communities of faith. The organizational logic of communities tends to reward visible activity and measurable outcomes — the programs that can be reported, the numbers that can be counted, the initiatives that can be evaluated. Belief in John's sense produces none of these directly. It produces abiding, which produces fruit, which cannot be manufactured by the organizational logic that rewards the appearance of production over the reality of relationship. The community that has genuinely received this lesson will look different from the outside than a community that has not — not necessarily less active but active differently, organized around the quality of its relationship with the vine rather than around the quantity of the fruit it is attempting to generate by its own effort.

The practical challenge of this lesson for individuals is equally searching. The temptation to substitute religious activity for the specific, sustained, relational engagement with Jesus that John calls believing is as available to individuals as to communities. The person who fills their life with religious content — with reading and study and service and attendance — while maintaining a careful distance from the actual encounter that genuine belief requires, is in the position of the crowds who follow Jesus across the lake for the bread rather than for the one who provides it. Jesus' response to them — you are looking for me not because you saw the signs but because you ate the loaves and had your fill — names the substitution precisely: they are oriented toward what

Jesus provides rather than toward Jesus himself, and the orientation, however sincere, is not the belief that produces life.

Lesson Three: Love Is the Evidence

John's third lesson is the one the new commandment most directly states, and the Farewell Discourse most extensively develops: the love that the community of Jesus' disciples practices for one another is the primary evidence of the Gospel's reality that the surrounding world has access to. By this, everyone will know that you are my disciples, if you love one another. The declaration is not primarily an exhortation to be loving as a general spiritual virtue. It is a claim about the epistemological situation of the watching world — about how the truth of the Gospel becomes visible to people who have not seen the signs and have not heard the discourses and who are therefore dependent on what they can observe in the community that carries the Gospel's name.

This lesson carries more immediate relevance to the contemporary situation of communities of faith than most applications of the love commandment acknowledge. The watching world in the contemporary moment is not primarily unconvinced by the intellectual arguments for Christian claims. It is primarily unconvinced by the gap between those claims and the observable quality of life and relationship in the communities that make them. The love that John's Jesus defines — the love of one who washes feet in full knowledge of betrayal, who lays down life for friends, who prays for those who are crucifying him — is recognizable when it is practiced as something the surrounding culture does not produce and cannot replicate. Its absence or distortion is equally recognizable, and its recognizable absence is among the most consistently effective arguments against the Gospel's claims that any skeptic has available.

The lesson presses on communities of faith not as a call to perform a more impressive version of the love they are already practicing but as a call to the honest examination of whether the love they practice corresponds to the standard the commandment sets. The standard is not warmth and goodwill. It is the cross — the love that gives without reserve and without condition, that is extended to those who will betray and deny and abandon, that moves toward cost rather than away from it. Every community of faith that takes this standard seriously will find it reorganizing its internal life at precisely the points where the surrounding culture's logic of reciprocal exchange pushes most consistently in the opposite direction. And every community of faith that finds itself in a credibility deficit with the world it is embedded in would do well to examine honestly whether the love it practices is recognizable to the watching world as the specific kind of love the commandment defines.

Lesson Four: The Paraclete Sustains What the Mission Requires

John's fourth lesson is the one that the Farewell Discourse presses most directly toward communities that are navigating the absence of the founding presence around which their common life was organized: the Paraclete — the Spirit of truth — sustains the mission in every generation, attending the community's engagement with the tradition, illuminating what the tradition means in new circumstances, and producing in each new generation the fruit that abiding in the vine makes possible. The mission does not depend on the physical presence of Jesus or on the living memory of those who knew him. It depends on the Spirit who was promised and who comes to those who abide in the relationship that the Gospel describes.

This lesson has specific and underappreciated implications for how communities of faith understand their relationship to the tradition they carry. The temptation in every generation is to choose between two inadequate responses to the tradition: either a fixed preservation that treats the formulations of previous generations as the final word and regards the Spirit's ongoing illumination as unnecessary, or a relativizing openness that treats the tradition as a collection of historically conditioned perspectives and regards the Spirit's ongoing illumination as license to revise without limit. John's promise of the Paraclete charts a different course: the Spirit will teach you all things and remind you of everything I have said to you. The tradition is not superseded by the Spirit's ongoing work. It is the substance of what the Spirit illuminates. And the Spirit's illumination is not the community's permission to say whatever seems adequate to the present moment. It is the opening of the tradition's meaning in the present moment in ways that require both faithfulness to what has been received and genuine openness to what has not yet been fully understood.

For modern communities of faith navigating genuine uncertainty about the tradition's application to circumstances that previous generations did not face, the promise of the Paraclete is both a resource and a demand. The resource is the assurance that the Spirit who attends honest, faithful, prayerful engagement with the tradition will illuminate what the tradition means in the new circumstances — that the community is not dependent on its own interpretive resources alone. The demand is the correlate of the resource: the community must actually engage the tradition honestly and openly, in the posture of those who expect to be taught rather than confirmed, if the Paraclete's promise is to be more than a theological formula applied to conclusions already reached by other means.

Lesson Five: Glory Comes Through and Not Around the Cross

John's fifth and most demanding lesson is the one that the passion narrative presses most directly and that the entire Gospel has been building toward from the prologue's declaration to the cross's completion: glory in John does not come after the cross as its reversal but through the cross as its fullest expression. The hour that Jesus has been moving toward throughout the Gospel arrives with the announcement that the Son of Man is to be glorified — and the glorification is the cross. The grain of wheat must fall into the ground and die before it can bear much fruit. The love that is declared in the prologue and demonstrated in the signs reaches its most complete expression not in a display of power that bypasses cost but in the specific, willed, complete giving of itself that the cross enacts.

This lesson is the one that every community of faith must receive afresh in each generation, because the temptation to locate glory in the demonstration of power rather than in the expression of love is perennial and takes new forms in every era. The community that is organized primarily around the demonstration of its own growth, influence, and institutional health — that measures its faithfulness by the metrics of visible success that the surrounding culture applies to every enterprise — is not organized around the pattern the cross defines. The community organized around the cross will look different: it will move toward cost rather than away from it, toward those whose need is greatest rather than toward those whose association is most advantageous, toward the forms of service that require genuine sacrifice rather than the forms that can be offered without real loss. It will measure its faithfulness not by visible outcomes but by the quality of its correspondence to the pattern of the one who declared it finished when the giving was complete.

The promise that accompanies this lesson is embedded in the image of the grain of wheat: the seed that falls into the ground and dies bears much fruit. The fruit is real, and it is the fruit of the dying rather than of a survival that avoids it. For communities that are willing to receive this pattern as their own — that are willing to give without reserve, to love without condition, to move toward cost as the natural expression of the kind of love the commandment establishes — the promise is the same promise Jesus made to his disciples in the upper room: that the fruit their abiding produces will last. Not the fruit of organizational effort applied to the production of visible outcomes. The fruit of a love that corresponds to the love the prologue declared and the cross enacted — the love that gives everything it has and declares at the end that the giving is complete.

What John Has Given to the World

The influence of John's Gospel on the history of communities of faith and on the intellectual history of the Western world is both pervasive and underestimated, in part because the Gospel has so often been read in isolation from its narrative structure — as a source of individual verses and theological propositions rather than as the sustained, carefully constructed argument about the identity of Jesus and the nature of belief that it actually is. The prologue alone has shaped the doctrine of the Trinity, the philosophy of the logos, the theology of the incarnation, and the understanding of revelation more decisively than almost any other single passage in the history of Christian thought. The Farewell Discourse has provided the primary vocabulary for Christian reflection on the Holy Spirit, on the nature of Christian community, and on the relationship between love and discipleship across two millennia of engagement.

The seven I am declarations have given the church its most concentrated and most demanding portrait of what Jesus claims to be and what believing in him makes available. The account of the man born blind has provided every generation that has read it with the clearest possible image of what genuine witness looks like and why it works: not argument but testimony, not the defense of a position but the honest account of an encounter. The Farewell Discourse has sustained communities navigating the loss of founding figures and the question of how the relationship with Jesus is maintained when the form it has taken is no longer available. The epilogue's restoration of Peter has addressed every community that has experienced the failure of its most prominent leaders and needed to understand what the resurrection does with failure rather than around it.

This does not mean that communities formed under John's influence have been consistently faithful to its vision. The Gospel that most explicitly presents Jesus as the light of the world has been used to cast darkness on Jewish communities across centuries of Christian anti-Semitism grounded in the misreading of its adversarial phrase the Jews. The Gospel that defines glory as the cross has been invoked to support institutional arrangements that look nothing like a servant washing feet. The Gospel that commands love on the standard of the cross has been applied in communities whose actual practice of love bears no recognizable relationship to that standard. Acknowledging this history is not a reason to abandon John. It is a reason to read it more carefully and more honestly — to allow the text to press its specific claims against the specific arrangements of each new generation with the same searching directness it pressed them in the first.

The Enduring Questions

The questions that John's Gospel raises cannot be finally answered by any human arrangement and will therefore continue to press themselves on every community and every individual in every era. They are questions about the incarnation — what it means that the Word became flesh, and what follows for the community that carries that claim about the embodied, physical, material dimensions of its common life. They are questions about belief — what genuine believing looks like in contrast to the religious activity that can substitute for it, and whether the community's actual life corresponds to the orientation toward Jesus that John's use of the word demands. They are questions about love — whether the love the community practices is recognizable to the watching world as the specific kind of love the commandment defines, and what the gap between the stated standard and the observable practice reveals about the community's actual formation.

These questions are currently being asked with unusual urgency in contemporary culture, because the institutions that previously provided frameworks for meaning, identity, and the organization of life around something larger than private accumulation have eroded significantly, and the hunger for genuine encounter — for a relationship with a reality that knows the actual person rather than the presented version, that offers life that death cannot terminate, that loves without the condition of adequate reciprocation — is everywhere evident in forms that range from the explicitly religious to the inarticulate. John's response to this condition is the same response it has always offered: the Word became flesh and made his dwelling among us, and those who received him were given the right to become children of God. Come and see. Come and believe. Come and discover that the life the Gospel offers is available now, in the specific texture of the present moment, to those willing to receive it by entering the relationship the Gospel describes.

The Character of Sustained Reading

Reading John well over a lifetime requires the cultivation of habits of reading that do not develop without intention and repeated return to the text across different seasons of life. The most important is the habit of bringing one's actual life to the text rather than the acceptable version — allowing the Gospel's consistent attentiveness to the interior of encounter to press on the interior of one's own engagement rather than managing the distance that keeps the text from reaching what it is designed to reach. John is not designed to be read as a theological reference work or a collection of memorable verses. It is designed to be read as the sustained, carefully constructed account of the one the prologue has identified, followed from the cosmic declaration at the beginning to the charcoal fire on the beach at the end, with the honesty and the attention that such an account deserves.

The reader who returns to John across different seasons of life will find that sustained engagement produces a specific kind of formation that cannot be achieved by any other means: not the mastery of Johannine theology but the gradual reorganization of the reader's interior life by sustained encounter with the one who already knows them — who knew Nathanael before Nathanael had spoken, who knew the Samaritan woman's history before she had offered it, who knows the reader's actual condition before the reader has brought the acceptable version to the text. This is the formation that the Beloved Disciple embodies: the recognition that comes before the explanation is complete, the arriving first, the seeing most clearly, that grows in those who remain close enough, long enough, and honestly enough to the one in whose presence those capacities develop.

The Permanent Invitation

The invitation that John extends across its twenty-one chapters is the invitation that the prologue announces and the epilogue confirms: come and believe, and by believing have life in his name. It is the invitation addressed to Nicodemus at night and to the Samaritan woman at noon and to the man born blind in the aftermath of his healing and to Thomas in the locked room and to Peter on the beach at dawn. It is addressed to people who come with their questions and their doubts and their failures and their grief, in the middle of their actual situations rather than from positions of spiritual readiness, and it extends to each of them not the expectation that they will arrive prepared but the encounter that reorganizes them from the inside before they have understood its full significance.

John was not written to produce people who have mastered the Gospel's theological content and are applying it with consistent adequacy to every dimension of their lives. It was written for communities navigating the same questions that every generation of the church has navigated: what does it mean to believe in someone you have not seen, to love in the way the cross defines, to abide in a relationship that cannot be seen or touched but that the Gospel promises is more real than the circumstances that press against it? For readers who bring to John the honest and sustained engagement it deserves, the most important thing the Gospel contains is not the sophistication of its Christological argument or the beauty of its literary architecture, but the encounter it makes possible — with the one who became flesh and dwelt among us, who loved to the end, who declared it finished from the cross, who stood in the garden at dawn and called a grieving woman by her name, and who stands now wherever the Gospel is read with the same question he has always been asking: do you believe this? The question has not changed. It does not change. And the life that genuine believing produces is, as John has been insisting from its first word to its last, the only life worth the name.

Closing Reflection

"Do you believe this?"
--- John 11:26 (NIV)

John's Gospel has endured because the claim it carries does not soften. In the beginning was the Word. The Word became flesh. Whoever believes in him will not perish but have eternal life. These are not claims that become more comfortable with familiarity or more manageable with the passage of time. They are the same claims they were when the prologue was first read aloud to a community in the late first century — radical, specific, demanding, and either true or not. The Gospel does not allow its readers to occupy a position between those two options for long. Its structure is designed to press toward the question that Jesus presses toward Martha at her brother's grave: do you believe this? The question does not change. The Gospel keeps asking it from its first verse to its last.

What gives John its lasting power is not the elegance of its prologue alone, though that prologue has shaped the intellectual history of the Western world more decisively than almost any other passage in the history of religious literature. It is the claim at the center of every sign, every discourse, every I am declaration, every encounter at a well or a grave or a breakfast fire on the beach: that the eternal Word who was in the beginning with God and was God has become what human beings are, has entered the human situation so completely that he could grow tired and weep and die, and has offered to those who receive him a life that the world did not give and death cannot take. This claim is either true, or it is not, and John does not construct its argument in a form that allows the reader to appreciate the claim without being pressed to respond to it.

One of the most characteristic features of John's Gospel, observed across the entire history of its reception, is its resistance to being received at a comfortable distance. The encounters it narrates are consistently unmanaged — arriving from outside the framework of expectation, cutting past the presented question to the actual one beneath it, pressing toward the interior of the person being encountered rather than stopping at the surface they are presenting. Jesus does not engage Nicodemus's opening compliment. He does not let the Samaritan woman's theological deflection redirect the conversation. He does not reassure Thomas after the resurrection by minimizing the demand for evidence. He presents the wounds and invites the touching, and then names the condition of every reader who comes to the Gospel after the first generation: blessed are those who have not seen and yet have believed. The invitation is not to a more comfortable version of the encounter. It is to the encounter itself, in the actual condition one is in, with the actual questions one is carrying.

John was written by a community that had lived with the tradition of the Beloved Disciple for decades, that had watched the eyewitnesses die one by one, and that was now writing for people who had not been there and would never be there — people who were dependent on testimony for the faith they were being called to. The explicit statement of purpose near the end of the Gospel is the honest acknowledgment of this situation: these things are written so that you may believe. The writing is the instrument through which the testimony reaches those who were not present, and the belief the writing is designed to produce is the same belief the signs produced in those who witnessed them and the resurrection appearances produced in those who saw the wounds. Not a lesser belief because it rests on testimony rather than sight. The same belief, pressed toward the same commitment, producing the same life.

Reading John well over a lifetime produces a specific and irreplaceable formation. Not the mastery of its Christological argument or the completion of its theological categories, but the gradual reorganization of the reader's interior life by sustained encounter with the one the prologue has identified — the one who already knows the reader better than the reader has yet brought to the text. The reader who returns to John across different seasons of life will find that the prologue they thought they understood yields something new when read from inside a season of genuine darkness, that the I am declarations press differently against different specific hungers, that the Farewell Discourse opens dimensions it withheld in earlier readings because those readings brought less of the reader's actual life to the encounter. The text is not exhausted by any engagement. It keeps depth in reserve for the honest reader who keeps returning.

The Beloved Disciple is the image of what this sustained engagement produces. He reclines next to Jesus in the position of greatest intimacy at the last supper. He stands at the foot of the cross when the other male disciples have gone. He arrives first at the empty tomb and believes before the explanation has been given. He is the first to recognize the risen Jesus on the shore of the Sea of Tiberias — before the catch, before the breakfast, before the restoration of Peter — and his recognition is the recognition of someone who has remained close enough, long enough, and honestly enough that the sight of the risen Lord through the morning mist registers before the others have fully woken. This is the formation that John is seeking to produce in the reader: not the sudden conversion of the uninformed but the deepening recognition of someone who has been present all along and who keeps arriving a little earlier, seeing a little more clearly, understanding a little before the explanation is complete.

The invitation that John extends is the same invitation it has always extended, from the prologue's declaration to the charcoal fire on the beach at dawn where the risen Jesus makes breakfast for people who failed him. Come and see. Come and believe. Come with your actual questions, your actual doubts, your actual grief, your actual hunger for a life more adequate than what the present world provides. Come as Nicodemus came, at night, with a half-formed question and more underneath it. Come as the Samaritan woman came, with a history that has been organized around a need that five relationships have not met. Come as Thomas came, demanding the wounds, receiving them, and finding that the demand was met with the specific evidence it required. Come as Mary came, weeping in a garden at dawn, hearing her name spoken by the one she thought was gone, and recognizing in the speaking of her name everything the Gospel has been building toward since the first verse. He is there. He has always been there. And the life he offers to those who receive him is, as John has been insisting from its opening word to its last, the only life worth the name.

The Bible for Modern Life Series

This book is part of **The Bible for Modern Life** series—an ongoing collection that explores the meaning, historical setting, and message of individual books of Scripture.

Each volume looks closely at the biblical text to help readers understand what it meant in its original context and how its truths still apply to life today.

The goal is simple: to help modern readers engage more deeply with the Bible—one book at a time.

— Samuel Whitaker